M000093349

Getting Started with Paint.NET

Create amazing images easily and professionally with one of the best free photo editors available

Andros T. Sturgeon

Shoban Kumar

BIRMINGHAM - MUMBAI

Getting Started with Paint.NET

First published: December 2013

Production Reference: 1181213

Published by Packt Publishing Ltd.
Livery Place
35 Livery Street
Birmingham B3 2PB, UK.

ISBN 978-1-78355-143-9

www.packtpub.com

Cover Image by John Quick (john.m.quick@gmail.com)

Credits

Authors
Andros T. Sturgeon
Shoban Kumar

Reviewer
Matt Penner

Acquisition Editor
Owen Roberts

Commissioning Editors
Sharvari Tawde
Priyanka Shah

Technical Editor
Dennis John

Copy Editors
Roshni Banerjee
Brandt D'Mello
Tanvi Gaitonde
Deepa Nambiar
Shambhavi Pai
Lavina Pereira

Project Coordinator
Akash Poojary

Proofreaders
Ameesha Green
Paul Hindle

Indexer
Mehreen Deshmukh

Graphics
Sheetal Aute

Production Coordinator
Kirtee Shingan

Cover Work
Kirtee Shingan

About the Authors

Andros T. Sturgeon is an average-sized human. His business card says that he is a futurist. He lives in Southern California, developing interactive experiences and original content for the Web. He is the founder of a transmedia agency named Starchild Interactive.

You can find out more about him via Google by searching for Andros Sturgeon or Starchild Interactive or by visiting www.starchild.us.

This is his first book.

Although writing is a solitary act, nothing is ever done without the assistance of others. I'd like to thank Packt Publishing and all of the people who helped in the creation of this book. A special thanks to Nathalie, because she is the most awesome.

Shoban Kumar currently works as a SharePoint consultant. In his free time, he develops open source desktop applications and Windows Phone apps. You can view all of his apps on his site at http://shobankumar.com.

He is an active contributor to the Stack Overflow forums and also runs a SharePoint blog at http://allaboutmoss.com.

You can follow him on Twitter via @shobankr.

About the Reviewer

Matt Penner is the Director of Information and Instructional Technology, CCTO, for the Val Verde Unified School District in Perris, California. In this role, he continues to grow a team that is passionate about excellence in service and works with other colleagues around the state to promote the building of successful technology support teams that people love.

Prior to this, he earned his B.Sc. degree in Computer Science from California Polytechnic University (Cal Poly) of Pomona, California, in 2002, and he has been a passionate advocate of software development for the last 20 years. He is an officer of the Inland Empire .NET Users' Group and was a frequent presenter at the Microsoft offices in Irvine, California, for the SQL Server 2008 launch and during the Windows 7 Phone launch events in the Inland Empire. He has been a professional small business consultant and still continues to moonlight with software development as and when time permits.

Matt has been a hobbyist graphics developer since Adobe Photoshop 2.0 in 1994 and has been an avid user of Paint.NET for over five years. Paint.NET is one of the few professional-level projects that continues to grow in ability and has a devout fan-following while still remaining free to download and use.

When he is not at work, Matt's other passions are his family. He enjoys spending time with his wife and three children and being involved in their church activities, little league games, music, games, and occasionally playing the prince at his daughter's imaginary castle.

> I would love to thank my wife and family, who are my rock and my island of sanity. Nothing would be worth doing without them to return home to. I'd love to thank Packt for this opportunity and the authors, Andros T. Sturgeon and Shoban Kumar, who put in the real time and effort to promote a great project they love and to write a book, making an easy tool even easier to master. Above all, I'd like to thank God, who gave me my family, my passion, and talents, and through whom I consider myself one of the most blessed individuals in the world.

www.PacktPub.com

Support files, eBooks, discount offers and more

You might want to visit www.PacktPub.com for support files and downloads related to your book.

Did you know that Packt offers eBook versions of every book published, with PDF and ePub files available? You can upgrade to the eBook version at www.PacktPub.com and as a print book customer, you are entitled to a discount on the eBook copy. Get in touch with us at service@packtpub.com for more details.

At www.PacktPub.com, you can also read a collection of free technical articles, sign up for a range of free newsletters and receive exclusive discounts and offers on Packt books and eBooks.

http://PacktLib.PacktPub.com

Do you need instant solutions to your IT questions? PacktLib is Packt's online digital book library. Here, you can access, read and search across Packt's entire library of books.

Why Subscribe?

- Fully searchable across every book published by Packt
- Copy and paste, print and bookmark content
- On demand and accessible via web browser

Free Access for Packt account holders

If you have an account with Packt at www.PacktPub.com, you can use this to access PacktLib today and view nine entirely free books. Simply use your login credentials for immediate access.

Table of Contents

Preface

Paint.NET is a free image editing tool available for the Windows operating system. Its user interface is very user-friendly and is similar to most of the popular paid image editing tools. Paint.NET can be used by both beginners and advanced users to create stunning images.

Even though it is not as powerful as the paid tools (for example, Photoshop), Paint.NET does a very good job. It can be used for most image manipulation tasks.

Plugins add more effects and functionality, thereby making Paint.NET one of the best free tools available.

What this book covers

Chapter 1, Welcome to Paint.NET, will cover a quick overview of Paint.NET, some of its functions, and how to install the program using a step-by-step approach.

Chapter 2, The Paint.NET Workspace, goes over the main window and functions of Paint.NET. It provides an overview of the main work area where we edit a picture.

Chapter 3, The Tools in Paint.NET, explains the different tools such as selection and move tools that are available in the main toolbar.

Chapter 4, Image Resizing and Editing, covers basic image editing, resizing, and removal of a background for advanced image processing.

Chapter 5, Adjustments, explains the various adjustment options such as Auto-Level, Hue, and Saturation that are available with Paint.NET.

Chapter 6, Working with Effects, covers all of the effects that you can apply to a photo. You will also learn how to apply effects differently to make your photo stand out.

Chapter 7, Working with Layers, covers how layers work in Paint.NET. You will learn how to merge different layers, delete layers, and how to adjust them.

Chapter 8, Supercharging Paint.NET, explains how you can extend Paint.NET using plugins to make it more useful. You will also learn how you can contribute to Paint.NET 's development.

What you need for this book

You will only need Paint.NET for this book. The latest version can be downloaded from http://www.getpaint.net/download.html.

Who this book is for

If you have ever wanted to create photos and images that go beyond simple point-and-shoot results, this book is for you. This book will help you create artistic images in ways that are limited only by your imagination. No prior knowledge of photo editing or editing software is required.

Conventions

In this book, you will find a number of styles of text that distinguish between different kinds of information. Here are some examples of these styles, and an explanation of their meaning.

New terms and **important words** are shown in bold. Words that you see on the screen, for example, in menus or dialog boxes, appear in the text like this: "For simplicity, choose **Quick Installation** and then hit **Next**".

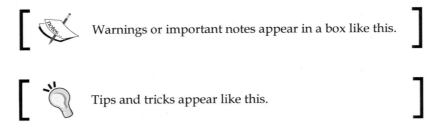

Warnings or important notes appear in a box like this.

Tips and tricks appear like this.

Reader feedback

Feedback from our readers is always welcome. Let us know what you think about this book—what you liked or may have disliked. Reader feedback is important for us to develop titles that you really get the most out of.

To send us general feedback, simply send an e-mail to feedback@packtpub.com, and mention the book title via the subject of your message.

If there is a topic that you have expertise in and you are interested in either writing or contributing to a book, see our author guide on www.packtpub.com/authors.

Customer support

Now that you are the proud owner of a Packt book, we have a number of things to help you to get the most from your purchase.

Downloading the color images of this book

We also provide you a PDF file that has color images of the screenshots/diagrams used in this book. The color images will help you better understand the changes in the output. You can download this file from https://www.packtpub.com/sites/default/files/downloads/1439OT_GraphicsBundle.pdf.

Errata

Although we have taken every care to ensure the accuracy of our content, mistakes do happen. If you find a mistake in one of our books—maybe a mistake in the text or the code—we would be grateful if you would report this to us. By doing so, you can save other readers from frustration and help us improve subsequent versions of this book. If you find any errata, please report them by visiting http://www.packtpub.com/submit-errata, selecting your book, clicking on the **errata submission form** link, and entering the details of your errata. Once your errata are verified, your submission will be accepted and the errata will be uploaded on our website, or added to any list of existing errata, under the Errata section of that title. Any existing errata can be viewed by selecting your title from http://www.packtpub.com/support.

Piracy

Piracy of copyright material on the Internet is an ongoing problem across all media. At Packt, we take the protection of our copyright and licenses very seriously. If you come across any illegal copies of our works, in any form, on the Internet, please provide us with the location address or website name immediately so that we can pursue a remedy.

Please contact us at copyright@packtpub.com with a link to the suspected pirated material.

We appreciate your help in protecting our authors, and our ability to bring you valuable content.

Questions

You can contact us at questions@packtpub.com if you are having a problem with any aspect of the book, and we will do our best to address it.

1
Welcome to Paint.NET

Paint.NET is a free, reliable program that rivals the most expensive photo editing programs on the market. Now, let us dive into the basic concepts of this software.

In this chapter will cover a general review of Paint.NET and what you need to do to get it, install it, and prepare it for use.

The topics covered are as follows:

- System requirements
- Downloading and installing Paint.NET

Nothing captures the attention more than an interesting image. If you take an amazing picture with any camera, chances are you will have to process it on some level. Whether you add a filter, change the color, or add an effect; a small change can turn an average image into a great one. Paint.NET is a Windows-based image editing program that gives you the ability to manipulate images professionally. It rivals similar software that can cost hundreds of dollars. The best part about Paint.NET is that it is a freeware, meaning it's completely free.

System requirements

The minimum system requirements needed to run Paint.NET are as follows:

- Windows 7 (recommended) or Windows XP
- .NET Framework 3.5 SP1
- A 800 MHz processor
- 512 MB of RAM
- More than 200 MB of hard drive space
- A 64-bit CPU and a 64-bit edition of Windows for 64-bit support (this is optional)
- A 1024 x 768 screen resolution

At present, there is no Mac version of this product.

Downloading and installing Paint.NET

To download Paint.NET, go to `www.getpaint.net/download.html`. In order for Paint.NET to pay a few bills and keep the servers going, the people who maintain Paint.NET have placed a few ads on the site that sometimes lead to other programs. You will most likely not want to download these programs. If you want to download only the Paint.NET program, make sure you click on the link that looks like the following:

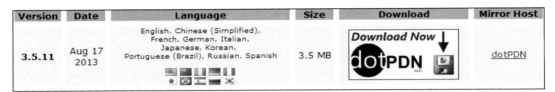

It can be rather confusing, so choose wisely.

Once you hit the correct link, it will take you to one of the Paint.NET mirror download sites. Hit the download link that looks like the following:

A ZIP file should begin downloading onto your computer. Once this is done, open the ZIP file and you will find a file named `Paint.NET.3.5.11.Install.exe`. Run this file and the installation will begin.

The installer will take you through a series of steps. For simplicity, choose **Quick Installation** and then hit **Next**. Read the terms and conditions, and if you agree to them, choose **I Agree** and hit **Next**. As the program installs, it will give you an opportunity to donate to the program if you wish. Because Paint.NET is a freeware, it only survives on donations and the time people put into it. So, if you like the program, donating here is one way to help out. When the software has finished installing, click on **Finish** and Paint.NET will open automatically.

Once the program launches, you will see a screen similar to the following screenshot:

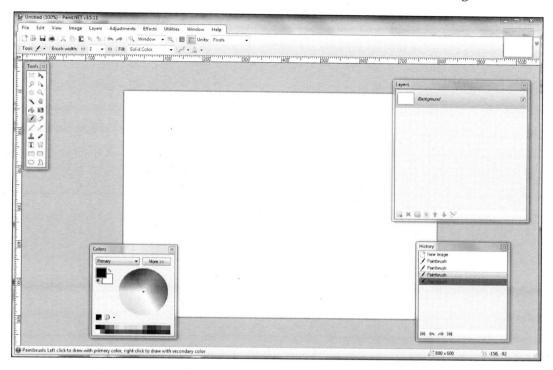

This is the entire Paint.NET work area. If you have used photo editing software like Photoshop, some of what you see in the preceding screenshot may look a bit familiar to you. If you are not used to an image editing program, all of these windows may look a little overwhelming. But don't worry, as in the following chapter, we will go over each of these windows and their functions.

Summary

In this chapter, we learned about Paint.NET and went over the minimum requirements of the software and how to install it.

In the next chapter, we will learn about the Paint.NET work area, the various windows associated with it, and how to open an image so you can start working on it.

2

The Paint.NET Workspace

Let us now get started and get acquainted with the workspace. In this chapter, we will go over the Paint.NET workspace and learn more about the program.

The topics covered are as follows:

- How to open and save an image
- Identifying the Paint.NET work area
- Finding out about different file types

Opening and saving an image

Let's start by importing a file to work with. There are several ways to open an image:

1. Drag-and-drop an image directly into the main workspace in the center of the screen and select the open icon on the menu bar:

Alternatively, select **File** | **Open**, or hit *Ctrl + O*:

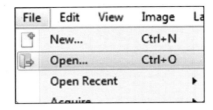

2. Once the image is imported into Paint.NET, save the image with a new filename. This is something I have learned the hard way. It only took me a few times of overwriting my original to realize I'd been working directly on the file I'd opened. When I'd made too many mistakes, I'd go back to the original to start over only to find that it no longer existed. Now I always make it a habit to create a copy.

3. To save an image, select *Ctrl + S* (**Save**) or *Ctrl + Shift + S* (**Save As**) to give it a new name:

4. You are now ready to work on your image. By importing a photo, the image size will automatically determine the canvas size. If you would like to create a file that is tailored towards a custom size, navigate to **File** | **New** or hit *Ctrl + N*:

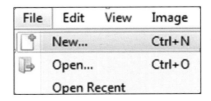

5. You will see the following window:

This window will pop up whenever you select **New**. It will give you the ability to choose how big you would like your final document to be. However, by default, if you copy and paste an image, Paint.NET will automatically create a document that is the exact size of the image from the clipboard, so there is no need to go though this process.

Now, if you ever want to save a step, just copy an image onto your clipboard and paste it directly onto a blank canvas. When you paste it, the canvas will default to the size of the image.

Work area windows

Let's take a look at the Paint.NET work area:

Paint.NET is comprised of a series of windows, each with their own function to help you with your workflow.

The following is a list of the various windows available on Paint.NET; the numbers correspond to the labels given in the previous screenshot:

1. The title bar
2. The menu bar
3. The toolbar
4. The image canvas
5. The Colors window
6. The status bar
7. The Layers window
8. The History window
9. The image list

The title bar

At the very top, we have the title bar. When you first open the program and before you import an image, the title bar will look like the following:

Once you open an image in Paint.NET, the title bar will look like the following:

The title bar will show you the name of the image that you're working on; in this case, that would be Motorcycle.jpg, the image we have imported here. The number in the brackets shows you the size of the image. Right now, this image is 22 percent of the actual size. This is followed by the version of Paint.NET you are working in. At the time of writing this, the newest version is 3.5.11.

The menu bar

Just below the title bar, we have the menu bar:

The menu bar gives you access to commands and menu items that you can use within the program. It's broken up into the menu and icons that represent common tools. We will go over the inner workings of the menu bar a little later.

The toolbar

The toolbar is the floating window that will first appear under the menu bar:

This is where you can select various tools that you will use to edit images. These tools are very similar to the ones that you will find in other image editing programs, such as Photoshop. Each tool has a different function and we will get into all of them a little later.

The image canvas

In the very center of the work area, we have the image canvas. This is the work area where you will view the image you are working on:

The Colors window

Below the **Tools** window is the **Colors** window. The **Colors** window allows you to select colors primarily when working with drawing and painting:

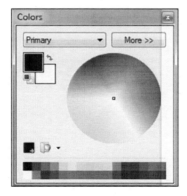

The status bar

The status bar gives you quick information about the project you are working on. On the left-hand side, it will tell you which tool you are working with (in this case, we are using the **Move Selected Pixels** tool). To the right, we have the image size (**800 x 600**) followed by the coordinates of the pixel your pointer is on. This window will also show you the rendering status:

The Layers window

Next we have the **Layers** window. This window will allow you to work with various layers within any file you are working on. We will go into how layers work later on. The first layer you work with will start at the background image by default:

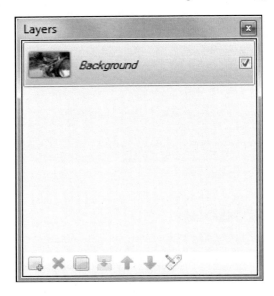

The History window

The **History** window allows you to look at various adjustments that you have made while working on your project. This is handy because it gives you the option to make changes to effects and adjustments you made several steps ago. As you work in Paint.NET, every action is recorded here, giving you the ability to go back in time and fix your mistakes:

The image list

The image list shows you small thumbnails of all the documents you are working on. This way, you can have several documents open and switch back and forth between them:

File types

Paint.NET uses the PNG, JPEG, BMP, GIF, TGA, and TIFF file formats, apart from its native file format, PDN. If you know what these formats are and when to use them, you can skip ahead to the next chapter.

The main type of file you will be using will be JPEGs, GIFs, and PNGs. Each one has its use depending on what you are using it for and are explained as follows:

- **Joint Photographic Experts Group (JPEG)**: This uses a type of compression that allows an image to be reduced in file size while preserving the quality. The problem with this particular compression method is the loss of information each time you edit and save the image. This is one of the most common types of files you will find on the Web as they are best suited for use as online photos because of how well they compress photos.

- **Graphics Interchange Format (GIF)**: Your choice of colors will be limited to an 8-bit palette or 256 colors. This is perfect for logos and charts—anything that doesn't require a lot of color depth. It has lossless compression, so your image will always look the same no matter what. Although it is considered an outdated format, it is still widely used. However, there are some people who prefer PNG, which is a newer alternative.

- **Portable Network Graphics (PNG)**: This allows for 16 million colors compared to GIF's 256. It was created as an open source successor to GIF. It's perfect for images that have large areas of uniform color. Another advantage is that it has its own alpha channel, that is, the ability to make different parts of an image invisible. This is handy for logos and other images where you want to place a background and let it show through. Some programs have trouble with PNGs and they may end up darker than originally intended. However, Paint.NET handles them just fine. The only drawback is that, because the image isn't compressed, PNG files tends to have a larger file size than JPEG files.

- **Other file formats**:

    - **Windows bitmap (BMP)**: This is a file format developed for the Windows environment. Although it is still used, it is not as widely used as JPEGs and PNGs. This format is not very popular because it is not compressed and not commonly supported in some web browsers.

    - **Tagged Image File Format (TIFF)**: This is another older file format not bound by any patents. It gained popularity due to its ability to handle multiple formats and for its lossless compression. However, newer formats have made this format a little outdated.

- ○ **Truevision Advanced Raster Graphics Adapter (TARGA) or TGA**: This is an older file format used on Windows OS. Its primary function, when it came out, was output for standard definition TVs. It was never intended for HD screens or print. Because of this, it not widely used.

- ○ **Native Paint.NET (PDN)**: PDN files can only be opened with Paint. NET and will not work in other programs. You can always save your images in this format and later convert them into any other format within the program. This is not an image type. Instead, it is a way to save your work.

Summary

In this chapter we got to know about the work areas in Paint.NET. This included the title bar, menu bar, toolbar, image canvas, Colors window, status bar, Layers window, History window, and image list. We learned what each of these areas is for and how to use them. In the next chapter, we will go over the tools in Paint.NET and how to use them.

3

The Tools in Paint.NET

This chapter covers the toolbar in Paint.NET and its functions. We will go over each tool in detail and how to use them.

The topics covered in this chapter are as follows:

- Selection tools
- Move tools
- View tools
- Fill tools
- Drawing tools
- Photo tools
- Text and Shape tools
- The Colors window
- Retouching a photo

The Tools window is where you will choose the different tools to work on your images. The Tools window is broken up into different categories. Each category is grouped together in a way that makes your workflow much easier. These are broken up into selection tools, move tools, view tools, fill tools, drawing tools, photo tools, and text and shape tools.

Selection tools

Selection tools are designed to allow you to select specific areas within your document so that you can perform activities like the color correction of effects. The following screenshot shows the selection tools available in the toolbar:

For example, let's say you took a photo and want to increase the contrast on somebody's face without affecting the entire photo. You can use one of the selection tools to isolate the area and increase the brightness of the face without changing the rest of the photo. The selection tools consist of the Rectangle Select, Lasso Select, Ellipse Select, and the Magic Wand. When these selection areas are active, they appear as light blue areas surrounded by small dashes.

Rectangle Select (shortcut key S)

As its name suggests, the Rectangle Select tool ▦ allows you to select a rectangle shape in your document.

This is perfect for areas containing sharp edges that you wish to isolate and change. When you select the Rectangle Select tool, your cursor will appear as a small cross symbol within the canvas window. Left-click on it and drag, tracing your desired area. As you do, you will see a blue-tinted square stretch across your selected area. Once you are satisfied with your selected area, release the mouse. If you are unhappy with your selected area, just start over. Your original selected area will disappear.

Lasso Select (shortcut key S)

The Lasso Select tool 🔎 will give you the ability to draw a freeform shape using your mouse.

This tool is perfect for areas you wish to isolate that have no hard edges. Like the Rectangle Select tool, you use it by placing your cursor over the spot where you would like your shape to start; left-click on your mouse and drag, tracing your desired area. Once you are happy with the shape you have created, let go of the mouse button. If you are unhappy with that shape, start again.

Ellipse Select (shortcut key S)

Similar to the Lasso Select and Rectangle Select tools, the Ellipse Select tool is perfect for creating uniform circles or ovals.

> When you choose the Rectangle Select or Ellipse Select tool, it will become longer or shorter depending on how you move it around. If you want to select a perfect circle or square, this can be done simply by holding down the *Shift* key. You will then be able to create a perfect circle or square.

Selection modes

As stated previously, selection tools allow you to select a particular area of your image; but what if you want to make more than one selection? What if the shape that you want cannot be achieved using just one of the tools? This is where selection modes come in handy. For example, you can use the Rectangle Select and Ellipse Select tools together using the Add (union) selection mode and create a completely different shape:

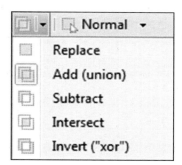

Replace

Replace is the default selection mode. This mode will replace any selection with a new one. For example, if you use the Rectangle Select tool and then use the Ellipse Select tool to select another area of the image, the area previously selected using Rectangle Select will be cleared and will no longer be available for processing.

Add (union)

The Add (union) selection mode will allow you to extend or add to an area you have already selected. For example, let's say you have selected a square area but you want to extend a small section of the area. You would use the Add (union) mode to do this. It will extend any area without changing the area you first selected.

The following screenshot shows a sample selection made using the Rectangle Select and Ellipse Select tools combined with the Add (union) selection mode:

Subtract

Subtract will remove the selected area that overlaps with the area selected with the first select tool. The following is an example of the Subtract selection mode being used with the Rectangle Select and Ellipse Select tools:

Unlike with the Add (union) selection mode, the area selected using the Ellipse Select tool removes the overlapping area that was selected using Rectangle Select.

Intersect

The Intersect selection mode does the opposite of the Subtract selection mode. It will retain the area that overlaps the area selected using any two selection tools.

Invert ("xor")

The Invert ("xor") selection mode will deselect overlapping activated areas. With this, you can add areas to your selection, but it will remove any other area you have previously selected.

Magic Wand (shortcut key S)

The Magic Wand tool ✎ is used to select areas of uniform color. Once you select the Magic Wand tool, place it on the area you would like to adjust. Simply left-click and an entire area will be selected. The Magic Wand tool works by selecting areas of similar color. How much area is selected can be determined by adjusting the Flood Mode and Tolerance level settings of the Magic Wand tool. The area selected will be highlighted in blue.

Flood Mode

Flood Mode has two different settings: **Contiguous** and **Global**. **Contiguous** will select all the nearby pixels that are similar in color, whereas **Global** will look for a particular color range across your entire photograph. How much of the selection is done will be determined based on the Tolerance level. The lower the value of **Tolerance**, the less sensitive the Magic Wand tool will be to the color of the pixel that was clicked:

Let us use the Magic Wand tool with the **Global** mode on the following image and see what happens:

If you notice, only the left-hand side of the image is selected even though there are other areas in the image that are similar in color.

In the following image, a larger portion with a similar color range is selected:

Move tools

After your selection is made, you can use Move tools to move the selected part of the image or the selection itself.

Move Selected Pixels (shortcut key M)

Use the Move Selected Pixels tool ➤ after you have selected an area in order to manipulate its size and rotation or cut it out completely.

This can be used in conjunction with any of the selection tools. The Move Selected Pixels tool is very handy if you wish to isolate an area within a picture and move or rotate it:

The section of the photograph in the previous screenshot is selected using Rectangle Select and then moved using the Move Selected Pixels tool. This tool will move the pixels to another area revealing the layer underneath the current layer.

Move Selection (shortcut key M)

The Move Selection tool ⇖ is handy if you want to move the selection to another part of the image.

Move Selection will not change the image. The following is a screenshot of a selection before and after the Move Selection tool has been used:

View tools

View tools let you change the way the image you are working on is presented to you in the workspace.

Zoom (shortcut key Z)

Use the Zoom tool 🔍 to zoom in (left-click) or zoom out (right-click) on a photo or area.

This is perfect for doing work on smaller or finer areas of a document. You can also left-click and draw a rectangle using the Zoom tool to zoom in quickly on a particular area.

Pan (shortcut key H)

Use the Pan tool ✋ to scroll or pan through an image.

This will save you a lot of time if you are zoomed in on a large document. You can access this tool at any time while working with other tools by hitting the Space bar. Whenever you hold down the Space bar, any tool you are working on will automatically become the Pan tool.

Fill tools

Fill tools allow you to fill a particular area of the image with a specific color and pattern.

Paint Bucket (shortcut key F)

The Paint Bucket tool 🪣 works similarly to other Paint Bucket tools in other graphics programs.

It works by selecting areas of similar color and filling them in with the color or pattern of your choice. The Paint Bucket tool has the Contiguous and Global flood modes, which work the same way as explained in the section *Magic Wand*.

Like the Magic Wand, it also has the Tolerance setting, allowing you to choose how sensitive the selected area will be.

Additionally, the Paint Bucket tool has three other settings not mentioned yet: **Fill**, **Antialiasing**, and **Blending**:

Fill

By default, you can fill an area with a color chosen in the Colors window. However, you can also choose various patterns to fill an area using the Fill drop-down menu. Using the toggle switch on the color wheel you can choose primary and secondary colors for these patterns. Using various colors and patterns you can create some very interesting effects.

Antialiasing

Antialiasing refers to how smooth your edges will be. With Antialiasing enabled, your Paint Bucket and Shapes selections will have much smoother edges by blending the edges with the neighboring pixels; however, the process will take longer to render due to the greater processing power it requires to do it:

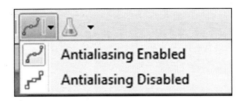

Blending

Next to Antialiasing, we have Blending. **Normal Blending** will blend each pixel into the new color if the chosen color has some transparency, but if the selected color is a solid color, the effect will be the same as that of **Overwrite**. This type of blending will replace the pixels with the new color you have chosen:

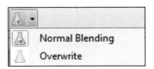

Gradient (shortcut key G)

Gradients  are gradual blends from one color to another. You can choose five different styles with the Gradient selection buttons.

The Gradient tool has other controls: Color mode and Transparency. Color mode will put a gradient over your entire image and is best used as a background layer. The Transparency mode will allow you to fade in your photo into other layers.

Start a gradient by left-clicking and dragging on a selected area. The gradient can be adjusted using handles that will appear in the form of small, moveable dots. The following screenshot shows a gradient with movable dots for adjustment:

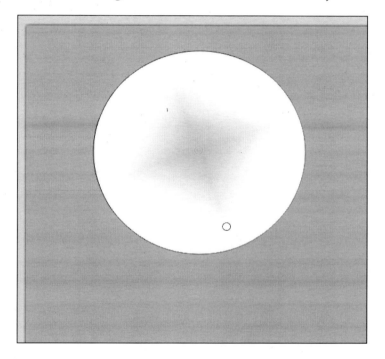

The Gradient tool also has a Blending mode that works the same way as mentioned previously:

Drawing tools

Drawing tools allow you to draw inside an image.

Paintbrush (shortcut key B)

The Paintbrush tool is the default tool when starting Paint.NET. It gives you the ability to draw freeform on your document using a mouse or a stylus. The value of Brush Width will determine how many pixels wide your brush will be.

> When you use the Brush tool, left-clicking will paint over the image with the primary color you've chosen from the color wheel. Right-clicking will paint over your image with the secondary color you have chosen.

Eraser (shortcut key E)

The Eraser tool will erase any part of the image you use it on, making it transparent.

This is good for erasing some backgrounds, but not as ideal as using the Magic Wand. The Eraser tool can be refined with its own Brush tool and Antialiasing.

> The checkered background you see when you erase part of a picture will not show up in your image. It is there to show transparent areas in your image.

Pencil (shortcut key P)

The Pencil tool ✏ allows you to draw one pixel at a time.

You can get almost the same result using the Paint Brush tool with a brush width of 1px and the Antialiasing disabled.

Photo tools

Photo tools are a set of useful tools that can be used for manipulating an image.

Color Picker (shortcut key K)

This tool ✎ is used to choose a color exactly as present in any part of your image.

The color you pick will be reflected in the color wheel. Left-click to choose the primary color and right-click to choose a secondary color.

Clone Stamp (shortcut key L)

The Clone Stamp tool ⚒ gives you the ability to take a region of a photo and copy those pixels and paste them onto another region.

This will be your go-to tool when fixing blemishes on a photo. You can use this tool by selecting the area you want to copy using *Ctrl* + right-click. Then, move your mouse to the area you want to fix. Left-click and move your mouse over it. Your two areas will stay equidistant from each other as you move your mouse. You can reset the selection by selecting a new area you wish to clone by using *Ctrl* + right-click again.

> If you want to remove a blemish from someone's face in a photograph, it's best to use the Zoom tool and get in as close as you can, then use a very narrow brush width. If you choose an area that is colored the same as the area the blemish is, you can easily give someone a clear completion with a few clicks.

Recolor (shortcut key R)

The Recolor tool ✎ will replace one color with another.

Using this tool, you can change the color of someone's shirt or the color of a car. It takes a little finesse to use it smoothly, but once you do, it can create some really interesting effects.

The first thing you want to do is select the color to which you are going to change your selection. You can do this using the Color Picker in the color wheel or by selecting the color from another part of your image by pressing the *Ctrl* key and moving the cursor to the area you want to select. Doing this will make the Recolor tool act like the Color Picker. You can choose your secondary color using *Ctrl* + right-click.

The secondary color in the Colors window is the one you want to replace. For instance, if you want to turn a blue sky red, hold down the *Ctrl* key and select the blue color of the sky. Select a secondary color in the Color Picker; use the Color Picker to choose the red color that you want to replace it with. Left-click and start painting the blue sky, and anything that is blue (the primary color) will be replaced with red (the secondary color). What's neat is that only the areas of the color you chose as your primary color will be painted. This can be adjusted with Tolerance. With this, Paint.NET will identify the edges that you are recoloring and the rest of your document won't be changed.

Text and Shape tools

Text and Shape tools allow you to draw geometric shapes and text on your image.

Text (shortcut key T)

The Text tool ⊓ allows you to put text on your image. It has the same controls that you have seen in other text editors. It also has the Fill utility, allowing you to add some interesting patterns to your text. Here, again you have Antialiasing and Blending (as discussed previously). To the bottom-right of your text, there is a small handle called the Nub. The Nub gives you the ability to move the text around to the exact spot you want. You can press the *Ctrl* key to make the Nub disappear so you can see what the text will look like without anything else on the screen.

Once you click on another area of your document, the text will become part of the image and cannot be edited. For this reason, it might be a good idea to always place your text on its own layer rather than directly on the image you are working on:

Line/Curve (shortcut key O)

The Line/Curve tool \|ℝ allows you to draw lines and curves. Once you select this tool, simply left-click and then draw the line from one point to another. Like other tools mentioned previously, you can use Brush Width to determine how thick you would like your line to be. You can also choose the style of line—solid or dashed—and choose the way the ends of the line will look.

In this example, I have created a dash-dot line with arrows on either side. You will notice small, pulsing boxes on the line itself. If you left-click on one of these squares, they will act as handles that curve your line any way you wish:

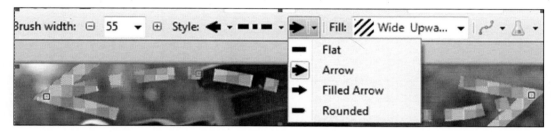

As with the Text tool, once you click on another part of your image, your line will become part of the image and you will not be able to edit it. For this reason, it is advisable that, as with text, you place the line on its own layer.

Geometric shapes

The remaining shape tools all function the exact same way and, similar to the Select tools, you can use the *Shift* key combination to draw uniform shapes. The one difference is the Draw Type selection. As shown in the following screenshot, you can select to draw a shape as an outline or a filled shape, or draw a filled shape with an outline. Your primary color will be the color of the shape; the secondary color will be the outline. As with the other tools mentioned previously, you can choose the type of fill pattern you would like to use.

The shortcut key for all of the shape tools is *O*. By repeatedly hitting the *O* key, you will be able to cycle through the shapes to select one of your choosing.

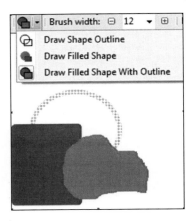

The three different shapes can be drawn in three different ways.

Rectangle (shortcut key O)

The Rectangle tool ▭ can be used to draw rectangles and squares.

Rounded Rectangle (shortcut key O)

The Rounded Rectangle tool ▢ can be used to draw rounded rectangles and rounded squares.

There are no in-built ways to change the corner radius for this tool, but there are plugins available to change the corner radius.

Ellipse (shortcut key O)

The Ellipse tool ⬭ can be used to draw ellipses and circles of various sizes.

Freeform Shape (shortcut key O)

The Freeform Shape tool ⬡ can be used to draw a shape with a freeform outline.

The Colors window

We have already covered the Colors window a little bit in this chapter, but here is a bit more information you may find useful. The primary color you choose will be the default color that will appear when using some of the tools mentioned previously. Use the small drop-down menu to go from primary to secondary color choices. You can select a new color by left-clicking anywhere on the wheel. You can also drag the dot in the wheel by holding down the left mouse button and moving it around. By clicking on the **More** button on the Colors window, you will see the values of your color choices. You can enter your own Hex number to choose the exact color you wish to use:

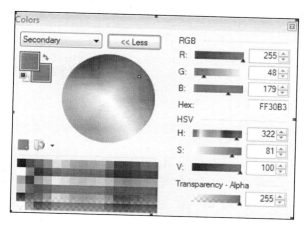

You can easily switch the primary and secondary colors by clicking on the double-headed arrow near the primary and secondary colors preview area. If you want the primary and secondary colors to change back to black and white, click on the small black-and-white button below the primary and secondary color preview area:

The **RGB** (Red Green Blue) option will determine how much of those primary colors you wish to work with or adjust.

The **HSV** option stands for Hue (the degree of a color), Saturation (how much of the color you want), and Value (how dark or light). Below that, we have the **Transparency - Alpha** slider. This slider will allow you to change how transparent the selected color will be. For instance, if you would like to have a box that is semi-transparent, use this slider to achieve the effect you want.

When creating shapes with color and transparency values, you must select your values first before you create the shape.

Finally, to the bottom-left corner of the Colors window, you have your palette selection. A palette is a selection of colors you can quickly select while working. When you first start Paint.NET, you are given a pallet of 32 of the most commonly used colors. However, you can create a custom pallet of your own colors by selecting a color on the Color Picker or entering a Hex value. The color you choose will be represented by a small square with a plus symbol at the bottom-left corner of the window, that is, the **Add Color to Palette** button. Click on the **Add Color to Palette** button and click on any square under it. The color you've selected will then be added to the palette.

You can save your custom palette by selecting the palette folder button to the bottom of the Colors window and clicking on the **Save Palette As** menu item. You can later load your custom pallet using the same menu.

Retouching a photo

Once in a while, we take that almost-perfect picture. Almost perfect because there may be that one thing standing out in the photo that ruins the image completely.

With a few simple steps, you can fix those problems and touch up a photo enough to make an average one look great.

The following is a photo that was taken for a real estate brochure. It's a nice pool, but the pool-cleaning pipe detracts from the aesthetics. I would like to remove that pipe altogether; let's see how we can do it using the tools we've learned about in this chapter.

Let us now follow some simple steps to do this.

Pool image before

Just remember, photo retouching is akin to digital painting in some regard. Sometimes it's easier, and other times you can make the "fixed" area look worse than what you were trying to cover up. Like anything, it's all luck. The more you do it, the luckier you will get.

For this you are going to use the Clone Stamp tool. As we learned in *Chapter 2, The Paint.NET Workspace*, the Clone Stamp tool replaces pixels from one part of your image onto another:

Pool image afterward

1. Select the Clone Stamp tool.

2. Select an area on your image that is most similar to the area behind the one you want to get rid of.

3. The area you select will appear as a circle with a plus symbol in the center. To the top-right corner of the plus symbol, you will see a small square. Press the *Ctrl* button and hold it down. The small square will turn into an anchor icon, meaning that this area is now anchored to the area we want to remove.

4. Left-click on your mouse and it will lock that section in.

5. Change the brush size. Experiment with the size that works best. Generally, you would want to use a smaller brush size to begin with.

6. Now select the portion of the photo you wish to remove.

7. You will notice that the place you anchored will be represented by a pulsing circle that will be the size of the brush you selected.

8. Left-click and start painting. You will notice that as you move your mouse, the anchored circle will move as well. This represents the cloned area the pixels are taken from.

9. If the area you are cloning appears too obvious, select a new area to anchor and continue the process. You may have to repeat this process several times if the area you want to remove is quite large or has lots of different shaded areas.

Pool image with hose removed using the Clone Stamp tool

With images, it's the details that make all the difference, especially when it comes to faces. A small blemish on someone's face is all it takes to destroy an impactful image. The same technique used for removing objects in a photo can be used to remove simple blemishes and scars. However, something to keep in mind is that human skin is a bit different. It has small and subtle nuances because of the way shadows and light play on the pores.

Summary

In this chapter, we learned all about the tools in Paint.NET. We learned about selection tools, move tools, view tools, fill tools, drawing tools, photo tools, text and shape tools, and the Colors window. We also used the tools learned in this chapter to edit a photograph and remove a part of it to make the overall image look better.

4
Image Resizing and Editing

In this chapter, we will learn about image resizing and editing. We will cover the very basics of how to make images smaller and larger, and will learn about canvas sizing and cropping. We will also see how to make a selection of an image and get it ready to turn it into a useable layer.

The topics covered are as follows:

- Rotating an image
- Cropping an image
- Resizing an image
- Resizing a canvas
- Creating selections
- Removing a background

Rotating an image

When you first start working on an image, you may need to change the orientation of it. This is common if you turn your camera sideways when taking the photo initially. This can be easily fixed by rotating the image. If you go to the menu bar and select **Image**, you will get options to reorient the image.

With the help of the rotate options, you can spin your image 90 degrees clockwise (shortcut *Ctrl + H*), counter-clockwise (shortcut *Ctrl + G*), or a full 180 degrees (*Ctrl + J*).

This is different from **Flip Horizontal** and **Flip Vertical**. These options allow you to create a "mirror image" of your photo. Using these will rotate your entire image; these options can be seen in the following screenshot:

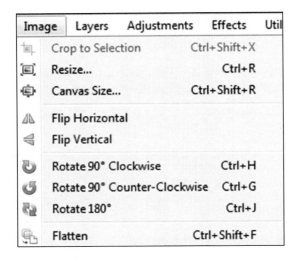

Flipping is different from rotating a layer. We will get more into layer properties in the next chapter.

Cropping an image

Let's say there is only a part of an image you want to keep or work on. In this case you will want to crop off the other part of the image. To do this, perform the following steps:

1. Select the tool of your choice: Rectangle, Lasso, or Ellipse.

2. Use the selected tool to draw your selection.

3. In the menu bar, select **Image | Crop to Selection** or use the keyboard shortcut *Ctrl + Shift + X*.

If this doesn't work, go to **Image | Crop to Selection**. If it is grayed out, make sure that you have something selected.

Resizing an image

As mentioned in *Chapter 2, The Paint.NET Workspace,* there is a difference between resizing your canvas and resizing your image. Your canvas size refers to the size of the document you are working on or the size of your finished document.

If you have imported a photo from a camera with a large sensor, for instance, an SLR camera, your image size will be very large because it will hold a lot of information. Most likely, you are not going to print an image of this size, so we will have to make it a little more manageable. First, we will want to resize the image to make it a little smaller:

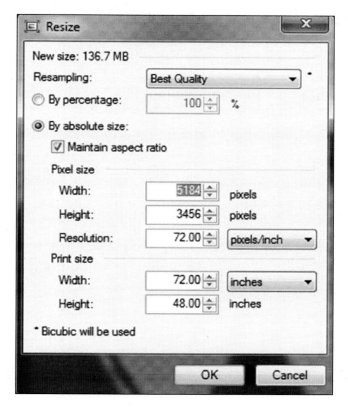

Because we opened the image first, Paint.NET sets the size of the canvas to the size of the image. As you can see, the image has a width of 72 inches and a height of 48 inches. An image of this size would be impractical if you were to print something like a flier on a standard sheet of paper.

So it is here that you can resize your image to something a bit more manageable. You can do this in the following two ways:

1. In the menu, select **Image/Resize** or use the *Ctrl + R* keyboard shortcut. This will bring up the **Resize** dialog box. Then perform the following steps:

    1. First, select how you want Paint.NET to resample the image or rearrange information in the image when you change the size. Usually, you will want to leave it on the default setting **Best Quality**. It will take more memory, but most modern systems can handle this.

    2. Under this option, you will notice two radio buttons: **By Percentage** and **By Absolute Size**. The **By Percentage** option will allow you to change your image by a percentage of what the original size is. By default, it is set to 100%. If we select this option, we can put in a larger value to make the image larger (for instance, 125%) or smaller (say 35%).

2. You can also change the size of an image by selecting **By Absolute Size** and entering custom pixel values for **Width** and **Height**. Perform the following steps to do so:

    1. Clicking on **Maintain Aspect Ratio** will automatically change your width if you enter a height value so the image won't become squished or distorted. Your height will automatically change if you enter in the width value.

    2. By deselecting **Maintain Aspect Ratio**, you will be able to change the image dimension as you wish; however, your image will most likely become distorted.

    3. If you prefer to work in centimeters, simply use the drop-down menu in this selection and change it from **inches** to **centimeters**.

Changing the image size

The image size and canvas size can be confusing for beginners. To make it easier for beginners to understand, consider the following image:

Imagine that you are painting on a white sheet of paper. This sheet is the canvas size and your painting is the image. If you want more space to paint more, you will add another sheet of paper to make it bigger. This will only increase the white space but not the size of the painting. Similarly, increasing the canvas size will give you more space but will not increase the image size.

Reducing the canvas size may affect the size of the image based on the change you make. For example, in the preceding image, if we were to reduce the canvas size to a value smaller than the image size, the following will be the result:

If you want your final document to be the size of, let's say, a standard sheet of letter paper, you will have to first adjust your image and then adjust your canvas size. Otherwise, your image will become larger than your canvas and the entire canvas will be filled with a closeup of one part of your image. The following screenshot shows you the options to adjust your image:

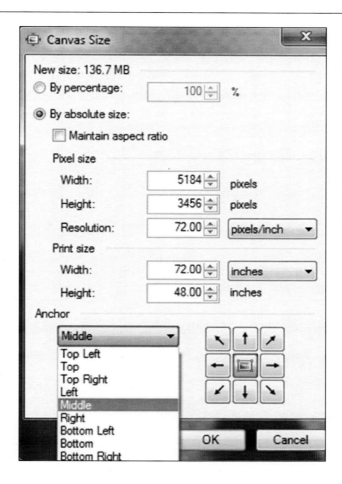

Resizing a canvas

Navigating to **Image | Canvas Size** or using the *Ctrl + Shift + R* keyboard shortcut will bring up the **Canvas Size** dialog box. This is where you will change the absolute value of your document. As with the **Image-Resize** dialog box, you can scale your canvas by a percentage or by the absolute values you select. You can also maintain your aspect ratio. You do this in the **Pixel size** option. However, you can select your print size, or what your final output will be with **Print size**. This means that you can work with a large version of your image, but when it is time to print, it will scale down your image to something more manageable.

Anchor points

An **anchor point** is the spot on your image from where the change should take place. To understand this better, consider the following image:

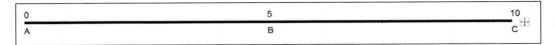

Imagine that the length of line AC is 10 centimeters. Point B is at 5 cm. If you want to increase the length of the line to 15 centimeters, there are a few options:

- You can draw a 5-cm line from point C. In this case, point C is the anchor point.
- You can also draw a 10-cm line from point B, and in this case, the anchor point is B.
- You can draw a 15-cm line from point A, and in this case, point A is the anchor point.

The same concept is used in canvas resizing.

Selecting an area

Selecting an area will give you the ability to isolate an area. Once you have the area selected, you can cut it out from your image, remove anything not selected, add an effect to the selected area, or change it in some way.

In the previous chapter, we learned about making selections with the selection tools. Now that you have learned how to make selections, let's get to work and see what you can do with them.

The following screenshot shows an image of a piece of art from the 2012 Symbiosis Festival:

Let's say that we would like to isolate just the artwork and erase the background to use on a flyer. There are a few ways to do this.

You could use something like the Rectangle Select tool to select just the artwork and the surrounding area and then navigate to **Image | Crop**. However, you will still have the sky in the background; this might be the time to use the Magic Wand tool.

Because there is so much contrast between the artwork and the background, we'll use the Magic Wand tool to select the areas that are lighter, like the sky.

Selecting with the Magic Wand tool

This can be done by performing the following simple steps:

1. Select the **Magic Wand** tool (shortcut key *S*).
2. In the **Selection Mode**, select **Add**.
3. Select your desired value for **Tolerance**.
4. Start clicking on the lightest areas and continue doing this until the desired area is selected.

5. If the value of **Tolerance** is too high and you need to undo a selection, simply hit the **Undo** button or use the *Ctrl + Z* shortcut, select a lower tolerance, and select the area again.

6. If you inadvertently select an area you don't want to remove, select **Remove** from **Selection Mode** and select that area.

Moving, cutting, or changing the selected areas

If you want to select a simple circle or square, just select one of the selection tools: **Square** or **Circle**. Considering you want to remove a round part of the sculpture, the following steps could be followed:

1. Select the **Circle** tool.

2. Drag a selection around the circle in the middle of the sculpture.

3. Use the **Move Selection** tool to fine tune your section if needed.

4. Select **Edit | Cut** or use the *Ctrl + C* shortcut to remove the selection.

5. Use *Alt* + left-click to subtract.

 If you hit the *Ctrl* key while selecting, you will select everything outside of your section.

Once you have selected the area you want to augment, you can also use the Select Pixels tool. It will automatically cut that selection out for you. Then you can drag it to another part of the image.

Selecting with the Lasso tool

Sometimes you may need to select an area freehand when Magic Wand doesn't work. This can be done easily using the Lasso tool.

To use the Lasso tool, perform the following steps:

1. Select the Zoom tool (shortcut key *Z*).

2. Select the Lasso tool. (shortcut key *S*).

3. Right-click and drag your cursor around the edge of the area you want to select.

4. Once the area is selected, you can cut it (**Edit | Cut** or *Ctrl + X*), which will remove the selected parts, or crop it (**Image | Crop to Selection** or *Ctrl + Shift + X*), which will remove everything but the selected parts.

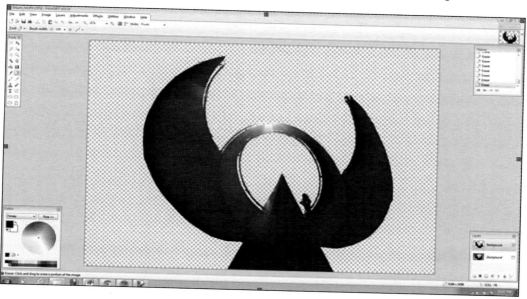

Once you have your selection, you can use this as a layer that you can manipulate and add to other layers.

In the next chapter, we will go over how layers work and how you can use them to give depth to your compositions.

Summary

In this chapter, we learned all about image cropping, image resizing, and canvas resizing. We also learned how to make selections in an image and remove the background. In the next chapter we will learn about adjustments and how you can add effects to your image.

5
Adjustments

This chapter covers the very basics of working with Paint.NET adjustments. We will go over how to work with an image's brightness, contrast, color adjustments, and levels.

The following topics will be covered:

- Auto-Level
- Black and White
- Brightness/Contrast
- Curves
- Hue/Saturation
- Invert Colors
- Levels
- Posterize
- Sepia

The following screenshot displays all of the options under **Adjustments**:

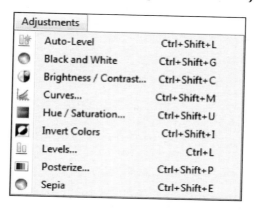

The **Adjustments** feature (*Alt + A*) of Paint.NET will be your go-to area to make simple corrections to your images. This is your one-stop shop for all corrections and enhancements, particularly with photos.

The nine adjustments listed here can be used in various combinations as well, further enhancing images. So, with a little bit of creativity, you can take an ordinary photo and turn it into an awesome photo. And who doesn't like awesome?

Auto-Level (Ctrl + Shift + L)

The Auto-Level feature is a very easy way to fix dark and light areas in your photos, fixing them instantly with the press of a button. Let's say you take a photo in a heavily shaded area on a bright day. You love the photo, but everyone's eyes are too shaded, and there is bright glare in other areas. What Auto-Level does is bring the light and dark areas into a normal range.

It does this by finding the darkest pixels and the lightest pixels and averaging them out. It may make the dark areas too light and the light areas too dark or give the entire image a muddy tone. You can also use this feature if you use the **Levels** feature and select **Auto**.

Now you try

You may now try using the Auto-Level option by performing the following simple steps:

1. Open a photo of your choice in Paint.NET.
2. Find the darkest area on the photo. Select one of the selection tools described in *Chapter 2, The Paint.NET Workspace* (Rectangle Select, Lasso, or Ellipse).
3. Select your chosen area with the tool.
4. Select **Auto-Level**.

 If Auto-Level does not quite work for your needs, you may need to make more precise adjustments using the **Levels** option described below it.

Black and White (Ctrl + Shift + G)

Black and White will remove all colors from an image, creating a dramatic effect. Once the color is removed from a photo, you can use another adjustment, such as **Levels** or **Brightness/Contrast**, to make the black pixels blacker and the white pixels whiter.

In this way, you can make a simple black-and-white effect pop in multiple ways.

Now you try

You may now try using the Black and White option by performing the following simple steps:

1.   Select one of your own photos and import it into Paint.NET.
2.   Select **Black and White**.
3.   Select **Auto-Level**.

Notice how doing these two simple things dramatically changes the tone of the image? You can take an average color photo of someone's face and turn it into a portrait just like that (snap!).

Brightness/Contrast (Ctrl + Shift + C)

Brightness/Contrast is a simple way to make colors in an image brighter or darker. It may be used to make the colors in an image brighter or darker or to make the colors stand out more or less than those around them.

If you move the **Brightness** slider to the right, all the pixels in the image will become uniformly brighter. Sliding it to the left will make all of the pixels darker:

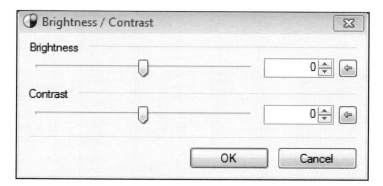

Contrast, on the other hand, will average out the pixels in the entire image. By moving the **Contrast** slider to the right, it will increase the difference between the lighter and darker pixels. Moving it to the left will make the dark and light pixels more uniform until they are nearly all the same.

Each of these options can increase or decrease by 100 percent of their original value. By playing with both the **Brightness** and the **Contrast** sliders together, you can make subtle changes to the photo that will eventually make your image stand out a bit more. You can reset your adjustments by hitting the small blue arrow to the right of the adjustment window.

However, if your image is really too dark or bright to begin with, the Brightness/ Contrast option may not work that well and will just make your image muddy.

If you do have an image that is very dark or bright, you might be better off using the Curves adjustment explained next.

Curves (Ctrl + Shift + M)

What Curves does is it allows you to adjust the amount of color and the luminosity (brightness) of each color shade within your image (red, blue, and green). This feature gives you a high degree of control in many aspects of your image. Because you can add ranges of adjustments based on intensity, you can use Curves to fine tune your image in ways that other adjustments can't.

The Curves interface

The Curves interface is an interactive grid that allows you to control aspects of an image with a simple line.

Horizontal values are the intensity input or the information going into the image and the vertical values are the intensity output or the information coming out of the image.

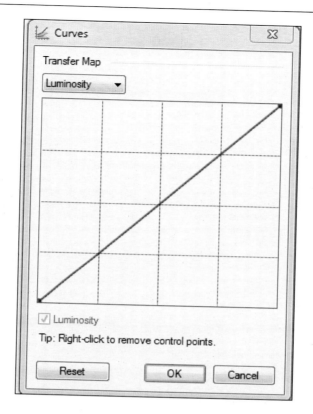

If you reshape the left half of the curve, it will affect the darker half of an image, and reshaping the right half will affect the brighter half. The diagonal line represents the image in its neutral position. If you move that line above the diagonal guideline, it will cause the affected areas to brighten. Moving that line below its default position on the diagonal guideline will cause affected areas to darken. The way the line bends is your curve.

You can then add control points by clicking on the area which is not already a control point. You can remove control points by right-clicking on the control point that you don't want. To move a control point, click-and-drag it to a new point.

Multichannel adjustments

Curves has two variables when using it. It uses the luminosity of an image to adjust the intensities of light and dark, and the other variable tweaks the **Red**, **Blue**, and **Green** channels. You can do this by selecting **RGB** from the drop-down menu.

Notice the **Red**, **Blue**, and **Green** checkboxes? By selecting or deselecting combinations of these, you can give a photo several different looks:

By changing the luminosity with Curves, you can reveal parts of an image that couldn't be seen before, such as the words on the main signboard and on the signboards behind it in the following image:

By changing the **Red**, **Green**, and **Blue** channels individually, you can completely change the look of a photo, transforming it into something really stylized.

Hue/Saturation (Ctrl + Shift + U)

The **Hue/Saturation** adjustment has three components—Hue, Saturation, and Lightness—as shown in the following screenshot:

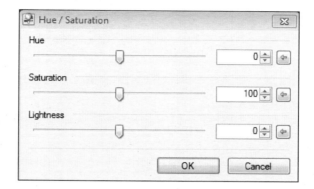

- **Hue**: This basically refers to the shades of a color available in the spectrum. It is the Hue that determines if there is a light blue or a violet blue. What the Hue does is switch or rotate the color spectrum behind the scenes. By using the **Hue** slider, you can change the color of everything in the image.

- **Saturation**: This refers to just how red you want your red and how blue you want your blue. Sliding the **Saturation** slider to the left will pull colors out until the image is black and white, while sliding it to the right will oversaturate your image with color.

- **Lightness**: This is how much "light" you will allow in your image. Sliding the **Lightness** bar to the left will let in less light until the image is black. Moving it to the right will add more until it is pure white. This is similar to brightness, but the algorithm it uses is different, making its effects more uniform.

Invert Colors (Ctrl + Shift + I)

Invert Colors does a twofold adjustment. It takes all the colors in the image and replaces them with their exact opposite on the color spectrum. Secondly, it will take the dark and light pixels and turn them to their opposite brightness. This will give your photo a negative photo or X-ray look.

Consider the following image:

After applying Invert Colors, the image would look like this:

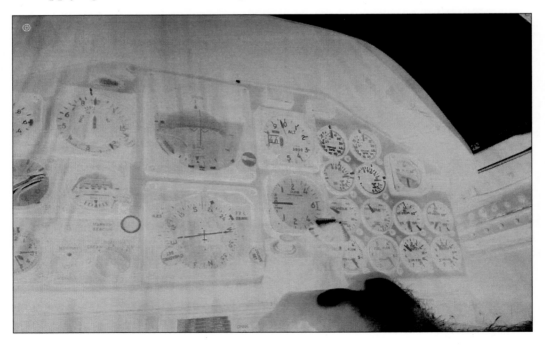

Levels (Ctrl + L)

Levels can change the color range or "exposure" of an image, including gamma or light adjustments. It can do this with individual color channels (red, green, and blue).

Levels duplicates the effect of increasing or decreasing the "exposure" of an image or how long the camera shutter is open. In the bygone days of film, the amount of light in the image was determined by shutter speed. The longer the shutter was open, the more light information was included in the final image. Too much light and you would get nothing but a bright white image.

Adjustments with Levels are done by adjusting the input and output of the white, black, and gray points. The white point is the brightest color that appears in the image. The black point is the darkest color. The gray point represents the average color of the entire image. With Levels, you can adjust all these points:

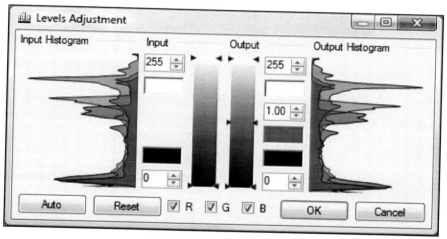

Levels has two parts: **Input** and **Output**. **Input** (on the left-hand side) represents your original image while **Output** (on the right-hand side) represents the image after your adjustment.

Notice the black and white boxes on the left-hand side? These are color swatches, each with a numeric representation. These can be adjusted using numeric inputs, the slider, or by double-clicking on the color swatches.

The small triangles are sliders that will allow you to change the light and the dark points of the image:

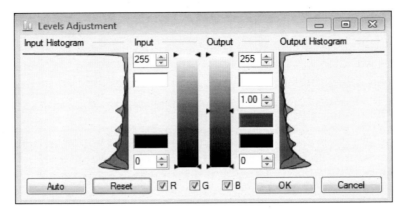

If you use the sliders on the left, they will fall or rise depending on where you are on that gradient. This represents the amount of lightness or darkness that will be going through the image.

Now, if you double-click on any one of the color swatches, you will see a color palette appear as shown in the following screenshot. This will allow you to change the color of the light let in either at the in point or the outpoint of an image. By doing this, you are telling Levels that any color in these boxes needs to be brighter or darker than the selected color:

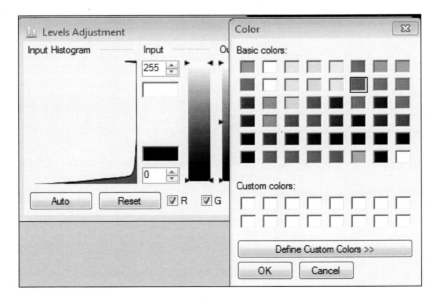

All adjustments are done on all channels (red, green, and blue). If you uncheck any of the RGB checkboxes, you can adjust just one color at a time.

The best advice given about Levels is just to play with it. You will find that the smallest of adjustments can make all the difference.

Posterize (Ctrl + Shift + P)

Posterize is an interesting effect that will decrease the number of available color values for each pixel. Normally, each color channel (red, green, or blue) will have 256 possible values, which means that there can be 256 shades of each. But **Posterize** will allow you to lower this range down to between 2 and 64. This will give your image a retro look, often associated with old posters:

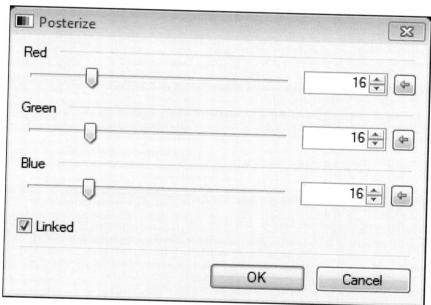

By default, this will start the red, green, and blue channels at 16 variables; using the slider on any one of these channels will slide the others as well, making all the color variables move together. If you wish to only lower the color variables of one channel, deselect the **Linked** option and you will be able to move the variables individually. The following is the appearance of the image before Posterize:

The following image shows the effect of posterizing with three colors:

Sepia (Ctrl + Shift + E)

Back in the early days of photography, when people used to take photos with a medium known as "film", chemicals were used to process pictures. Color film did not exist in those days, so the world was black and white. The chemicals used were a bit unstable, making some pictures degrade after only a few years. To keep this from happening, silver sulfide was used to make photos last longer. However, this would give the black-and-white photos a brown tint known as "sepia".

Today, we still associate photos with this tint for an old photo look. Thankfully, you don't have to expose yourself to toxic chemicals in your photo processing; you just have to hit the **Sepia** button. This will instantly give your photo an aged look.

To do this, simply hit *Ctrl + Shift + E* or navigate to **Adjustments | Sepia** from the main menu.

The following is the appearance of the image before applying Sepia:

The following image shows the same photo after applying Sepia:

Summary

In this chapter, we learned all about the adjustments of Paint.NET. We learned about the Auto-Level, Black and White, Brightness/Contrast, Curves, Hue/Saturation, Invert Colors, Levels, Posterize, and Sepia adjustments. We learned that with very small adjustments, you can take an average photo and dramatically change it into something outstanding.

6
Working with Effects

This chapter will cover the effects of Paint.NET. It will go over basic image manipulation and the application of various special effects to images.

In this chapter we will learn about the following effects:

- Artistic
- Blurs
- Distort
- Noise
- Photo
- Render
- Stylize

One of the most interesting and robust parts about Paint.NET are the effects. The effects are broken up into seven categories: **Artistic, Blurs, Distort, Noise, Photos, Render**, and **Stylize**. These are shown in the following screenshot:

Every image actually tells a story. Even very small adjustments can help bring focus to parts of the story you wish to tell. By combining effects with adjustments along with a little creativity, you will be able to accentuate the story you are telling; making it more alive than it would have been otherwise.

You will find yourself using some of these effects quite often, while others you may never use. I, however, recommend experimenting with all of them.

A word of warning

Some of the effects can be very memory-heavy. This means that adding some effects may take a while to render. If you have an older computer or laptop, chances are you are going to have to wait a minute or two with each adjustment.

It is best to resize the image to a smaller size by navigating to **Image** | **Resize** from the menu or using the *Ctrl + R* shortcut and then taking the image down to something more manageable so you won't end up using many resources. A standard DSLR camera will create a very large image. If you are saving it for the Web, as a general rule, reduce the size of the image before adding any effects, unless your computer has large amount of memory.

Artistic effects

There are three **Artistic** effects: **Ink Sketch**, **Oil Painting**, and **Pencil Sketch**. You will notice that some of these effects work much better on some images than others. While one effect may give you its intended effect on an image, it may just look strange on other images.

Ink Sketch

Ink Sketch will take your image and give it the look of being drawn by a black ballpoint pen. This effect is limited to black only, so if you want to use another color, say red, it will be rather difficult. You can combine other effects and adjustments to this effect, but some adjustments and effects won't work on top of it (**Sepia**, for instance, won't do a thing to the photo if added after **Ink Sketch**).

Ink Sketch has two adjustments: **Ink Outline** and **Coloring**, as shown in the following screenshot:

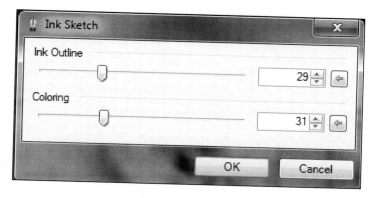

Ink Sketch works by figuring out the outlines of the image and replacing them with dark lines. **Ink Outline** determines how much attention **Ink Sketch** pays to those edges with the ink outline. This is similar to the tolerance for the other tools. It has a value between 1 and 100. The lower the number, the lesser edges it will see, and vice versa, filling in the smallest lines and shadows.

Coloring will add in the original colors from the image between the dark lines. As with **Ink Outline**, **Coloring** has a value between 1 and 100. The higher the number, the more color it will add and vice versa.

Oil Painting

Oil Painting is meant to convert your image into a replica of an oil painting. It can pull this off sometimes; at other times it will end up making your image look blotchy and uneven. How well this effect works depends on your photo and on what your idea of an oil painting is.

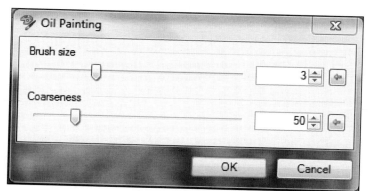

Oil Painting has two controls: **Brush Size** and **Coarseness**.

Brush Size has a value between 1 and 8, 1 being the finest brush, which hardly has any effect, and 8 which looks like it could be a horse's tail. The larger the number, the more it will replicate a brush with more thickness.

Coarseness represents how "thick" you would like your "oil paint" to be. **Coarseness** has a value between 1 and 255. The smaller the number, the thinner the paint. A larger number is meant to replicate very thick paint.

Pencil Sketch

Pencil Sketch is meant to replicate what your image would look like if sketched by a lead pencil. The **Pencil Sketch** effect will remove all color from the image and trace the lines with gray, pencil-like lines. This gives it a much softer look than **Ink Sketch**, but sometimes, it looks more like a black-and-white copy of your image rather than an actual pencil sketch. **Pencil Sketch** has two controls, as shown in the following screenshot:

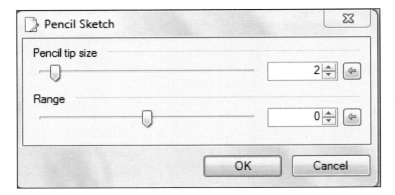

The **Pencil tip size** has a value between 1 and 20; 1 being the sharpest, finest point, and 20 being the thickest.

Range has a value ranging from -20 to 20. This determines how much of the photo will be "in pencil". This works just like the tolerance in many tools.

Blurs effects

Some blur effects can come in handy in numerous ways. Other blur effects you will find have an interesting effect, but may not serve any of your purposes.

The Blurs effect menu has seven different effects: **Fragment, Gaussian Blur, Motion Blur, Radial Blur, Surface Blur, Unfocus,** and **Zoom Blur**:

Fragment

The **Fragment** blur will create fragments of your image in small chunks based on a value of your choice and then zoom these fragments with another value of your choice:

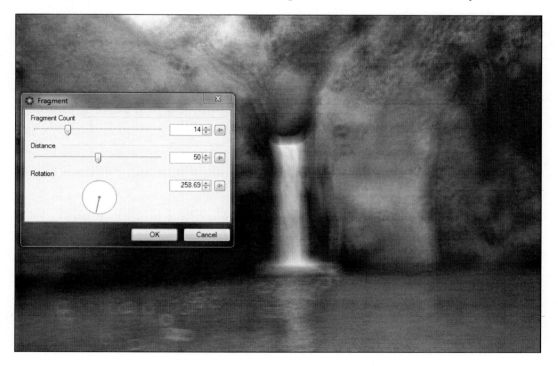

As shown in the dialog box in the preceding screenshot, **Fragment Count** is the number of fragments that will be created, and the **Distance** is the value of how far these fragments will be placed. **Rotation** is the direction in which these copies will be moved.

Gaussian Blur

Gaussian Blur is probably going to be your go-to blur effect if you want to add a simple blur to a layer or an image. It can come in handy if you just want to soften an image a little or use it around a background to bring more attention to your subject.

Use a **Gaussian Blur** effect with the Lasso tool to create a false depth of field. **Radius** determines the amount of blur applied to your image.

Motion Blur

Motion Blur will take a perfectly fine in-focus image and turn it into an image that looks like you snapped it out of a moving car. If used carefully, it can make your image come alive with action.

Radial Blur

The **Radial Blur** effect will be very handy if you wish to create a blur around a person or object while keeping your subject in focus. This is an incredibly handy tool for to create a point of focus or a vignette. What this will do is draw attention to your subject in a very unique way.

Radial Blur has three controls: **Angle**, **Center**, and **Quality**.

The **Center** control, as shown in the following screenshot, will pop up in a few of the effects explained later and is really easy to understand.

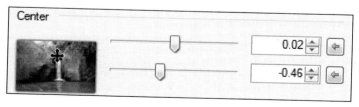

The **Center** control works on an X/Y grid. By moving the levers, you can center the + symbol on the section of the image where you would like your blur to originate. Keep in mind that if you are working with a large image, it may take some time to render the image completely. Keep an eye on the bottom-right of the **Project** window, and you will be able to see how the rendering process is progressing.

Surface Blur

The **Surface Blur** effect will put a very thin blur over the entire image. This will give your image a "soft focus" effect. This comes in very handy to soften an image. If your subject has wrinkly, leathered skin, this simple effect is the equivalent of a face lift. It smoothes out wrinkles and hard lines and makes the image softer. This is a technique that has been used since the time that films were used, and is achieved by smearing petroleum jelly on the lens. Now you can achieve it by hitting a button and save your lens from the smears!

Surface Blur consists of two controls: **Radius** and **Threshold**:

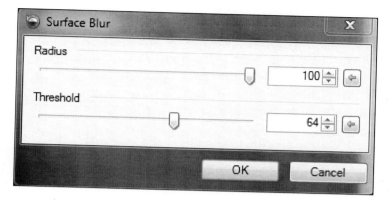

Radius, which has a value between 1 and 100, represents the size of the area you would like to blur, 1 being the least and 100 being the most. Think of this as a shutter closing around the center of the image.

Threshold also has a value between 1 and 100. This represents the amount of blur you wish to add. The higher the number, the more blur you will add. Adding too much may make your image look smeary, but with the right combination of **Radius** and **Threshold**, it can really give someone a glamorous look.

Unfocus

Unfocus does exactly what its name implies; it makes a focused image lose focus at a certain point. This may come in handy if you wish to blur out a background while working with layers. **Unfocus** has a value between 1 and 200, 200 giving you the maximum blur:

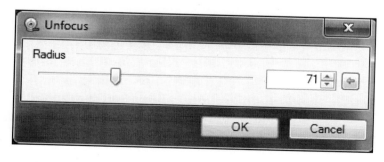

Zoom Blur

Zoom Blur works just like **Radial Blur** and is a really good standby for creating vignettes. While Radial Blur makes an image look like the outer edges have been spun, **Zoom Blur** makes it look as if you were zooming into the subject when the photo was taken. This makes the area around your subject blurry, keeping the center in focus.

Zoom Blur has two controls: **Zoom Amount** and **Center**. **Zoom Amount** has a value between 0 and 100. The higher the number you select, the more it will appear blurred around the edges. **Center**, like **Radial Zoom**, will allow you to choose where you wish the point of focus to be. The radius cannot be controlled and hence your may be limited. For instance, if you have a close-up of someone's face, you may find that your subject's eyes are in focus while the mouth may be out of focus. This may end up giving you the effect you want, depending on your intention, but using **Radial Blur** may be better as you can control the radius with it.

Distort effects

Distort has eight different effects: **Bulge**, **Crystalize**, **Dents**, **Frosted Glass**, **Pixelate**, **Polar Inversion**, **Tile Reflection**, and **Twist**. These will add crazy special effects to your photos, so try and see what each of these do because they will enhance your creativity:

Bulge

Bulge creates funhouse distortions that can add comical effects to images. Although, you may find that you can use it to correct some imperfections as well.

Bulge has two controls: **Bulge** and **Center**. **Bulge** has a value between -200 and 100. 0 is neutral or no bulge at all; anything under 0 will make the center of the bulge smaller or make that part appear distant. Anything over 1 will make the bulge bubble larger or make the image appear closer.

As with other effects covered in this chapter, the **Center** control will allow you to place the bulge where you would like it to be.

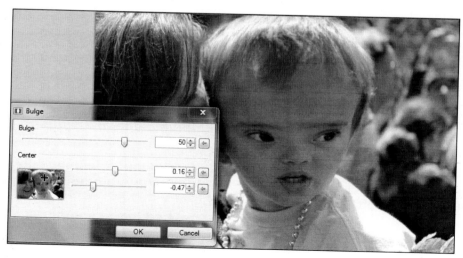

Dents

Dents has six controls: **Scale**, **Refraction**, **Roughness**, **Tension**, **Quality**, and a **Reseed** button for **Random Noise**:

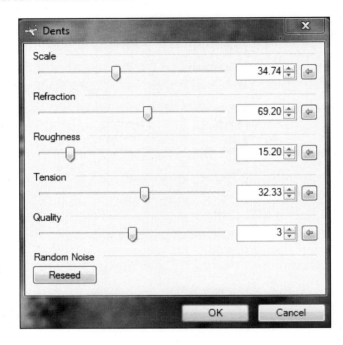

If your image is a sheet of steel, the controls are a hammer you will use on it.

Scale determines how many times the "hammer" hits the steel. **Refraction** determines how reflective your steel is. **Roughness** lets you control how polished the steel is. **Tension** represents how tightly packed the hammer hits are. If at any point in time you don't like the way the "hammer hits" are laid, you can hit the **Reseed** button and get a new layout.

Frosted Glass

Frosted Glass will make your image look like its being seen though a sheet of frosted glass.

Frosted Glass has three controls: **Maximum Scatter Radius**, **Minimum Scatter Radius**, and **Smoothness**. It works by scattering pixels randomly. You can choose the maximum or minimum value that you wish the randomness to be.

Maximum Scatter Radius determines how far the "frost" crystals are from one another. It has a value between 1 and 200. The larger the number, the more it will scatter each pixel.

Minimum Scatter Radius will determine the minimum randomness that the pixels are scattered by. The **Minimum Scatter Radius** also has a value between 1 and 200. It will always be limited to the value of **Maximum Scatter Radius**. You will not be able to bring the value of **Minimum Scatter Radius** higher than that of **Maximum Scatter Radius**.

Smoothness determines how grainy you want the frost to be. It has a value between 1 and 8. The higher the number, the less grainy it will appear:

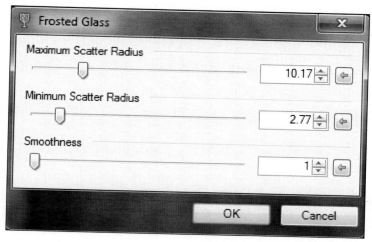

Pixelate

The **Pixelate** effect will lower the resolution of your image. It has a value slider that ranges from 1 and 100. The higher the number, the lower the resolution and the larger it will make each pixel. It averages out the pixels in the surrounding area and will change the surrounding pixels to that color:

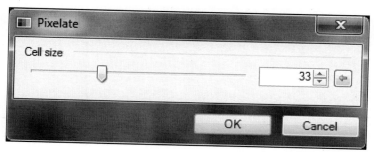

With the Ellipse Selection tool, **Pixelate** lets you recreate scenes from your favorite police reality shows:

Polar Inversion

The only way to describe **Polar Inversion** is psychedelic. It will take the bottom of the image and wrap it around to the top, repeating this multiple times based on the variables you select:

> Using **Polar Inversion** improperly may result in opening a portal to another dimension.

Tile Reflection

Tile Reflection will make your image look as if it's covered with reflective tiles. It has four controls, namely, **Angle**, **Tile Size**, **Curvature**, and **Quality**:

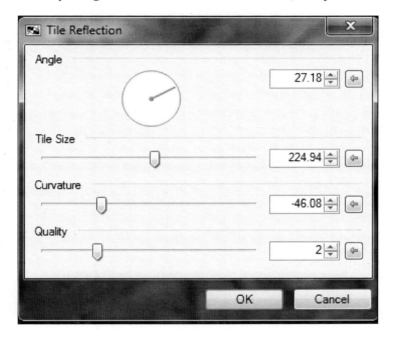

Angle controls how the tiles are angled, **Tile Size** controls how large the tiles are, and **Curvature** will create the illusion of raised, reflective tiles:

How did this kid get that cool tiled shirt? With Magic Wand and **Tile Reflection**!

Twist

The **Twist** effect will take any area of your photo and start twisting it as much as you want. The **Center** control works as with other effects mentioned earlier. **Amount/Direction** determines how much spin you wish to give your photo. **Size** will determine how big/small the spin ball will be. **Quality** will give finer detailing to the "spin ball":

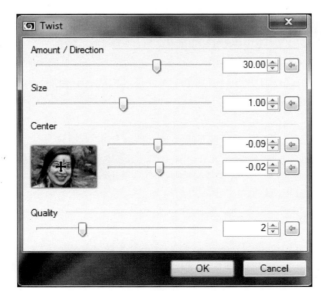

By using the Ellipse Selection tools with **Add** mode and adding a twist to each instance, you can create some rather interesting effects. And by interesting, I mean disturbing.

Noise

Noise effects can be hard to figure out. On one hand, it's impossible to think why you would want to add noise or random grain to any photo, but there are times it comes in handy. Let's say you were on a vacation with your friends. You have a very good camera, while your friends have the BoxMart $69.99 special. One of your friends wants you to put together a photo album of your adventures. Only, your photos look way better than anyone else's. You may need to make your image a little less sharp so it doesn't stick out so much against the others. Okay, that's probably not going to happen to anyone, but you get the idea. Sometimes an image is just too sharp and **Noise** will do the trick.

Add Noise

Add Noise will add random pixels of red, blue, green, and yellow. As shown in the following screenshot, the **Add Noise** effect has three controls: **Intensity**, **Color Saturation**, and **Coverage**:

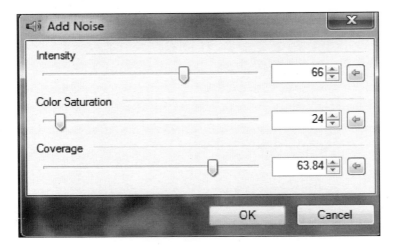

Intensity determines how bright those random pixels will be. **Saturation** allows you to saturate these random pixels with more color, making the red redder and the green greener. **Coverage** will determine how many of these random pixels will appear. The greater the value, the more "noise" you will see:

Adding Noise with a Black and White adjustment turns a photo into something resembling a newspaper photo. You may now be asking yourself, "What's a newspaper?"

Photo effects

Photo effects are grouped together as the effects you will probably use most to enhance your photos. The grouping makes sense as you will see later. You may find yourself going here more than to any other grouping to make adjustments to your photo:

There are four photo effects: **Glow**, **Red Eye Removal**, **Sharpen**, and **Soften Portrait**.

Glow

Glow is a real great way to give any photo a dream-like quality. What it does is make the bright areas of the photo glow with a golden aura. It has **Radius, Brightness**, and **Contrast** as controls. The higher you adjust these levels, the more glow you will give your image:

Red Eye Removal

There isn't much to say about **Red Eye Removal** except that it removes red eyes in flash photos. It detects the reddest parts of a photo and removes it. As it says in the controls of this effect, it works best to isolate the eyes using selection tools. If you don't, it can create interesting results sometimes.

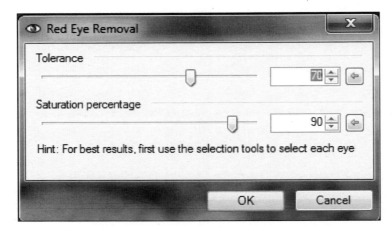

Sharpen

Sharpen only has one control and only does one thing. However, the sharpening it does is marginal. If you are expecting it to save your out-of-focus photos, you are not in luck:

Soften Portrait

Soften Portrait is a great effect. It combines **Surface Blur**, **Glow**, and **Saturation** into one easy package. The controls for this effect are **Softness**, **Lighting** and **Warmth**. **Softness** works similar to **Surface Blur**, **Lighting** has the same functionalities as **Glow**, and **Warmth** works a little bit like the **Hue** adjustment. With a few simple adjustments, you can really make your photos pop:

Render effects

There are only three **Render** effects: **Clouds**, **Julia Fractal**, and **Mandelbrot Fractal**. It's hard to figure out just what to do with **Render** effects. But, if you are geeky like me, you will love them:

Clouds

Out of these three effects, **Clouds** is the one you will probably find the most use for. It doesn't really make clouds. What it does is render a cloud-like image based on a mathematical algorithm, which you will need an advanced math book to understand. For our purposes, you don't need to know how it does it, but just need to know what it does.

Clouds has three controls: **Scale**, **Roughness**, and **Blend Mode**. When you first employ it, your image will disappear completely and be replaced by some grayish clouds. **Scale** will give you a zoomed view of those clouds. **Roughness** will determine how soft or hard you want your clouds to look. It is the **Blend Mode** that makes things interesting.

Blend Mode will allow you to blend the clouds you create with your photos in very interesting ways. There are 14 blend modes and not enough space in this chapter to explain what each one does. But there is space to explain that each one will blend the clouds into the picture in a different way. Then, using the **Scale** and **Roughness** sliders, you can further change the way the photo looks.

The **Reseed** button will change the formation of the rendered clouds if you aren't happy with their placement.

Honestly, using this effect has so many variables that it's impossible to describe how it will change the look of each of your images. The best way to really see what it does is to play with it. The following screenshot shows the 14 modes of **Blend Mode**:

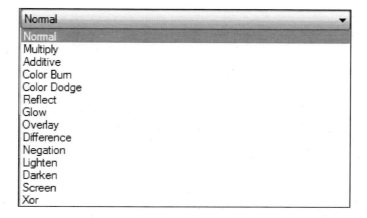

The next question is, why would one use this effect? You can use it to create a fog effect in an image or to add texture to a background layer and make it a bit more complex. You can add colors or other effects to make your image more stylized. This is an area where you should just start stacking different blend modes, effects, and adjustments and see what you can come up with. If you don't like something you added, you can always go into the **History** window and remove whatever you don't like.

Julia Fractal

Fractals are visual representations of mathematical formulas. The subject of fractals is a very complex one, and there are many books on the subject written by people far smarter than me.

Julia Fractal and **Mandelbrot Fractal** (discussed in the next section) replace your image with a colorful image, as shown in the following screenshot. The controls **Factor**, **Zoom**, **Angle**, and **Quality** work in the exact same way as the controls in the other effects covered already.

Apart from creating a really cool image, **Julia Fractal** doesn't do much; however, you could use it to create some interesting layered effects.

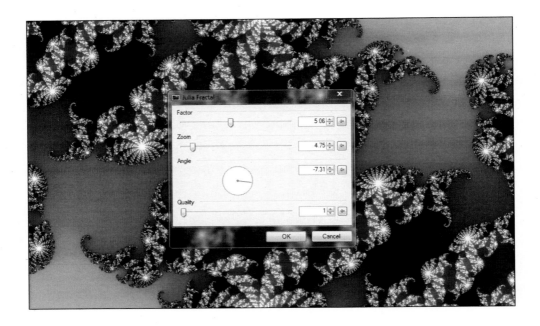

Mandelbrot Fractal

Like **Julia Fractal**, **Mandelbrot Fractal** uses a mathematical equation to create an interesting image:

Trapped within **Mandelbrot Fractal** lie all the secrets of the known universe. Now contemplate infinity until you slowly go insane.

Stylize effects

All **Stylize** effects do the same thing; they detect the edges of your image and accent them in various ways. **Stylize** has four effects: **Edge Detect**, **Emboss**, **Outline**, and **Relief**.

By detecting the edges and highlighting them, it can give your images an interesting 3D quality:

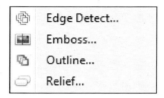

Edge Detect

Edge Detect has only one control: **Angle**. This determines the angle of your edges. **Edge Detect** will remove all the color from your image except for the color within the edges:

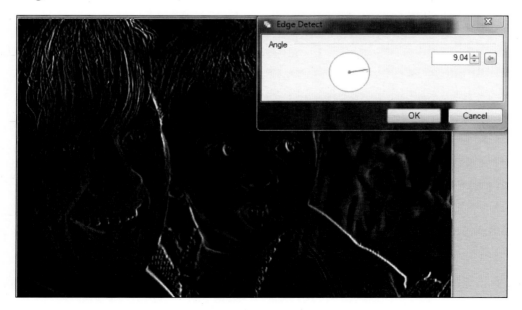

Emboss

Emboss also has **Angle** as its only control. It turns your photo into a gray-scale image but makes all the lines look raised or embossed.

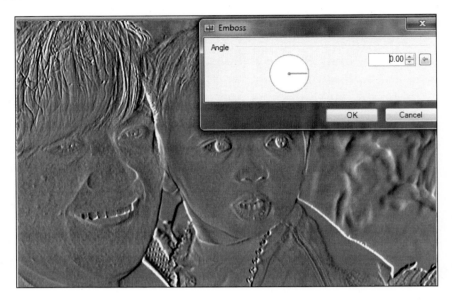

Outline

Outline takes all the edges of your image and turns them black against a white background. It has two controls: **Thickness**, which controls how thick the black outlines will be, and **Intensity**, which determines how intense the edges of the black line will be.

Relief

Relief leaves the color of your image intact but "raises" the image lines just like **Emboss**. This will give your image a little texture, but it can also make your image look a little bit like you have slight double vision:

Relief also has **Angle** as its only control.

Summary

In this chapter, we learned all about the effects that you can use to manipulate your image. We learned about the **Artistic** and **Blur** effects to bring focus to a particular part of your image, the **Distort** effect to make someone look funny, the **Photo** effects to make a photo better or create interesting images.

7
Working with Layers

In this chapter we will go over working with layers within Paint.NET. Here we will cover the very basics of how layers work, and how to make them work for you. We will cover the best way to use layers and avoid some common mistakes. We will also create a simple project using layers.

The topics included are as follows:

- How layers work
- Adding a new layer
- Merging layers
- Deleting a new layer
- Moving a layer up or down
- Adjusting a layer

How layers work

Up until now, we have gone over the various ways we can change the look of a single image. This is great for one or two corrections. But let's say you have an isolated part of a picture and want to drop it into a different background. Trying to work on the same image will be next to impossible, especially if you want to change the color or effect on one of its parts. That is why you will need to work with layers.

Think of layers as sheets of glass. On one sheet of glass, you place a cutout of your friend's image. You will not only see your friend's image, but you will also be able to see content present on the other layers of glass. If you take a random background, you can put it on another sheet of glass and place that sheet behind the image of your friend.

Now it looks like your friend is standing in front of the new background. You now have two layers. So let's say you want something to appear in front of your friend. You would do this by adding another layer and placing it on top.

Adding a new layer

By default, Paint.NET will assume that the first layer you have opened is your background layer. The background layer will always be the one at the very bottom. This layer will also be a solid layer and by default, will not be transparent.

We are going to start a new project by using a simple background. Then, we are going to use the Paint Bucket tool to turn the entire canvas blue. This will serve as the background for our image:

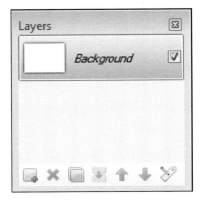

Next, we will hit the icon that adds a layer. This is the small square icon with a plus symbol at the extreme left-bottom of the screen. This will add another layer to the image we are working on, and our **Layers** window will look like the following:

Notice that it looks like nothing has happened? That's because the new layer is transparent. It will remain transparent until you start adding something to it. If you look at the **Layer** window, there are check marks next to each layer. This determines if the layer is visible or not. For now, we will uncheck the blue background layer, and when we do that, we will only see the new transparent layer.

The first thing we are going to do is use the Line tool to start creating a sunburst pattern. We don't want our line to be too big, so we will go for a line width of 10 pixels. We do this by drawing lines as if we were slicing a pie. We will also turn on the Ruler tool in the menu bar so we can get a better idea where each line should go:

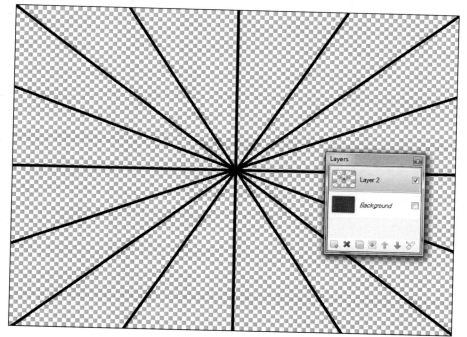

Because we are working on a specific layer (in this case **Layer 2**) anything that we do to this layer will not affect the blue layer underneath, which is currently invisible. This is great in case we mess up, because the layer underneath will not be touched and we won't have to start over.

Once this is done, we will use the Paint Bucket tool to fill every other section with color. This will give us a fairly good sunburst pattern. Reselect the blue layer and voilà!

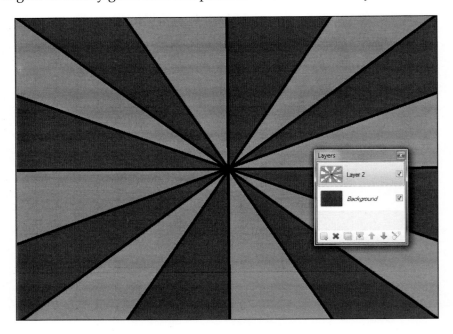

The only problem is that it looks a little too crisp and bright. In order for it to not overshadow the rest of the image, we will want to tone it down a bit. So we are going to add something else. A good way to do this is to add a bit of grunge, also known as a texture:

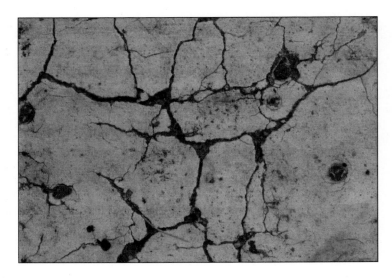

Textures are layers that add subtle elements to your images. Anything can be used as a texture. Concrete, brick walls, dirt, stones, and a rusty sheet of metal all work well. A texture can be anything that has some sort of consistency without pulling your focus to any one part of the image, and it's easy to create your own textures.

You can find all sorts of textures online. We are going to use this cracked paint texture and add it to the top layer:

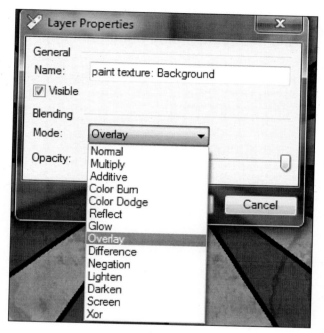

Double-clicking on any layer will show us the **Layer Properties** dialog.

The **Layer Properties** dialog allows us to change the name of the layer. While working with many layers, it's easy to get confused with different layers and their content; so it's better to rename every layer with a meaningful name that will help you quickly identify the content of the layer.

We can also change the **Blending** mode. **Blending** modes allow us to choose how the layer blends into the next layer. By default, this is **Normal**, meaning that the layer will just lie on top without any changes. But if we use the drop-down menu and change the **Blending** mode to **Overlay**, the Grunge layer will seem to blend into the bottom layers.

Each of these **Blending** modes will do this in different ways, and it would take more room than we have here to explain them all. To learn more about each blending mode, visit the *Blend Modes* page in Paint.NET's help guide at http://www. getpaint.net/doc/latest/BlendModes.html.

You will find that you can use different blending modes with different layers, giving you extra creative options.

Merging layers

Too many layers might get a little too unwieldy. So what we are going to do now is merge the layers into one. Doing this will give us only one layer that is easier to deal with. Since these three layers will serve as our background, we will use them as one from here on. We will start with the very top layer and merge it down:

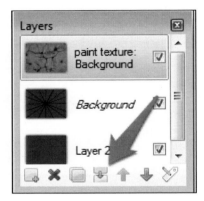

We will rename this new layer merged layers. This is now one unified layer that we will be able to control as a whole.

Now we are going to take the art piece image we created in *Chapter 4, Image Resizing and Editing*, in which we removed the background. However, we don't want to have the grunge layer affect this layer, so we are going to put this on the top layer.

We do this by navigating to **Layers | Import From File...**:

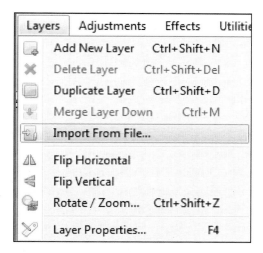

In the pop-up window, navigate to the location where we saved the file and import the image by clicking on **Open**:

Only, something weird happens here. If you notice, the background has suddenly become a thumbnail. Why is that?

When we first worked on this photo and removed the background, we were working with a very large file and we had saved it without resizing it.

If you are importing another layer, by default, Paint.NET will change the canvas size to the largest size layer.

What we will have to do in this case is select the layer we want to resize in the **Layers** window. Then, using the Select tool, grab the bottom-right corner of the layer and shrink it down so it fits into the background layer. Once the Sculpture layer is resized, resize the canvas back to the original size we were working with. In this case, 800 x 600 pixels:

Now, on closer inspection, we see that there are still some pixels that are visible even after we removed the background. We can see them much better, now that there is our background showing through. We are now going to use the Eraser tool and remove the extra pixels. This is easy to do because the Artwork layer is on its own and erasing the extra pixels will not affect the layers below it. The following is our resulting image:

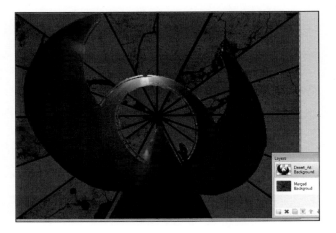

Adjusting a layer

Now that is looking pretty good! But we want to start adding some effects to it to give it a bit more style. What we want to do now is duplicate the Artwork layer. We do this by navigating to **Layers | Duplicate layer**, selecting *Ctrl + Shift + D*, or by selecting the **Duplicate Layer** button on the **Layers** window.

Now we have a second instance of the Artwork layer, one on top of the other, and we are going to add an effect to the layer beneath the first.

The next thing we want to do is add an effect. We are going to add the **Frosted Glass** effect (**Effects | Distort | Frosted Glass**):

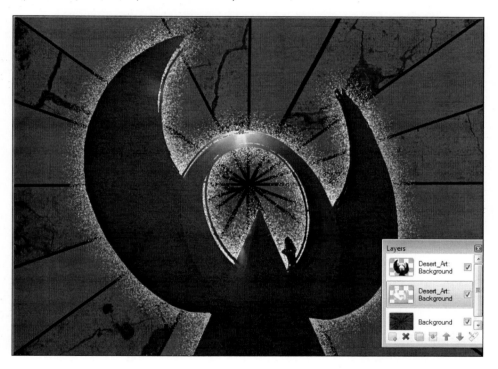

This effect only happened on the duplicate layer. I spared out the refraction just a bit, so now it has this really interesting effect:

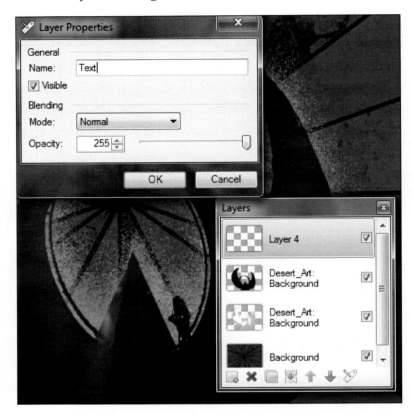

We are now going to create another layer. Double-click on the layer, get the layer properties, and rename this layer to Text Layer. On this layer, we are going to write Welcome to Paint.NET.

Now, one thing to keep in mind is when we write that text, before we do anything else, we need to adjust the color, size, and font of the text. One of the shortcomings of Paint.NET is the inability to edit text once we have created it, so it's important to set our parameters first.

If you don't like the Text layer, you can select the layer and hit the red X symbol, which will delete the layer.

Moving layers

The next thing we want to do is make the text look like it's behind the artwork, but not behind the Frosted Glass effect.

We are also going to add an effect called a **drop shadow** to the text to add depth. Drop shadows are handy adjustments that make text (or any other image) look like its hovering above the layer below it. It's subtle, but it does the trick and makes things come alive when used correctly.

Finally, we are going to move the Text layer down one level. We do this by selecting the Text layer and hitting the down arrow key on the **Layers** window. This will bring our text under the main layer, but in front of the **Desert Art** duplicate layer that has the Frosted Glass effect:

Summary

In this chapter, we learned how to work with layers, and how to merge, move, and apply effects to individual layers. In the next chapter, we will learn about Paint. NET plugins, how and where to get them, and how you can contribute to the development of Paint.NET.

8

Supercharging Paint.NET

This chapter covers the ways that you can make Paint.NET even more powerful by installing some free adjustments and effects.

The topics covered in this chapter are as follows:

- Plugins in Paint.NET
- Getting plugins
- Helping yourself if you get stuck
- The top five plugins to get
- How you can make Paint.NET better

Plugins in Paint.NET

Plugins are small bits of software that extend the functions of a program. Most software, whether it's a web browser or a full graphics suite, has plugins that extend the function of the original program.

Plugins available for Paint.NET are of two types:

- **File types**: These plugins extend the types of files that can be opened and processed in Paint.NET
- **Effects**: These plugins add more effects and adjustments that you can apply to your images

Getting plugins

Getting plugins for Paint.NET is super easy. In the menu bar, navigate to **Help |
Plugins**. Once you select **Plugins**, a new web page will open in your default web
browser. Make sure you are connected to the Internet.

It will take you to `http://forums.getpaint.net/index.php?/forum/7-plugins-
publishing-only/`.

Here, you will see a long list of plugins. To install a plugin, simply copy the extracted
files from the plugin ZIP file to the `Effects` folder in the Paint.NET folder. This is
usually `C:\Program Files\Paint.NET\`:

If you get stuck, read the post **HOW TO INSTALL PLUGINS**. It will take you through a step-by-step process. This takes a little time, but it is super easy.

Helping yourself if you get stuck

As mentioned previously, Paint.NET is free. This means that there is no tech support of any kind.

So, where do you go if you run into any problems or need help? Under the **Help** tab in the menu bar, you will notice that there are several sections. Three of them that will help you the most are mentioned in the following sections.

Help

Help Topics (*F1*) will take you to the help topics website found at `http://www.getpaint.net/doc/latest/index.html`.

This web page is a one-stop shop for everything about Paint.NET, starting from installation to details about every window in Paint.NET.

Forum

Forum is an excellent, well-maintained source of information about everything that has anything to do with Paint.NET. It has years of archived postings of people helping each other with the program. There are probably no issues that haven't been dealt with here. It's all searchable; so if no help topics seem to give you the answer you are looking for, it is most likely that you will find the answer here. The forum can be found at `http://forums.getpaint.net/`.

Tutorials

Tutorials is the best place to go if you want to really stretch yourself with Paint. NET. There are lessons and tips galore. It is here that people upload projects they completed with Paint.NET, and then they break down exactly how to recreate them. It is a great place to go to get inspiration. The site can be found at `http://forums.getpaint.net/index.php?/forum/18-tutorials-publishing-only/`.

The top five Paint.NET plugins

There are many plugins to choose from. It's hard to know exactly which ones may suit your personal needs. Some plugins do amazing things, while others seem to be of little use at all. This list is not definitive by any means. It is, however, a good roundup of some of the more interesting ones. This, of course, is a matter of preference. Your list may look a little different depending on your preference.

Pyrochild plugins

Pyrochild plugins is a series of 20 plugins that will greatly enhance your creative flow. The developer asks for a $6 donation, and it is well worth considering this based on what it does. The plugins can be found at `http://forums.getpaint.net/index.php?/topic/7291-pyrochild-plugins-2012-9-16/`.

MadJik' all plugins

MadJik' all plugins is a pack of 60 plugins, which are far too numerous to list here. There are many plugins here that do interesting things to your photos. They can be found at `http://forums.getpaint.net/index.php?/topic/7186-madjik-all-plugins-last-updated-2012-01-01/`.

BoltBait's plugin pack

The BoltBait's plugin pack has 21 plugins and a palette file that give you a lot of toys to play with. The developer asks for a donation of $6. That's about $0.35 a plugin, which is not a bad deal. BoltBait's plugin pack can be found at `http://forums.getpaint.net/index.php?/topic/8318-boltbaits-plugin-pack-updated-december-12-2011/`.

The Photoshop PSD file plugin

The Photoshop PSD file plugin allows you to save and open Photoshop files. This plugin makes Paint.NET cross-platform and very powerful. It can be found at `http://forums.getpaint.net/index.php?/topic/18128-photoshop-psd-file-plugin-newest-version-230/`.

The dpy's pack

dpy's Pack is another large pack of plugins, including some really nifty text effects. It can be found at `http://forums.getpaint.net/index.php?/topic/16643-dpys-pack-2012-08-26/`.

How you can improve Paint.NET

At the end of the day, the main core of Paint.NET is maintained by one main person: Rick Brewster. He maintains a blog about the future versions of Paint.NET, which can be found at `http://blog.getpaint.net/`.

If you are a developer and would like develop plugins or contribute to the development of Paint.NET, you can find developer-related information at `http://forums.getpaint.net/index.php?/forum/17-plugin-developers-central/`.

If you happen to stumble upon any bugs or issues, you can always send an e-mail to `feedback@getpaint.net`.

Above all, the thing that will help the most is donating. Rick Brewster maintains the core of this software for free, as a service to the world. Now, because you don't have to spend $300 for a similar software, buy Rick a sandwich or something bigger if the spirit moves you. You can make your donations at `http://www.getpaint.net/donate.html`.

Summary

In this chapter, we learned how to supercharge Paint.NET with plugins, where to get help if needed, and how you can help the developers keep Paint.NET free for everyone.

Index

H

History window 17
HSV option 37
Hue/Saturation adjustment
  about 63
  components 63
Hue/Saturation components
  Hue 63
  Lightness 63
  Saturation 63

I

image
  anchor point 50
  canvas, resizing 49
  cropping 44
  opening 9-11
  resizing 45-48
  rotating 43, 44
  saving 9-11
image canvas 15
image list 17
Image-Resize dialog box 49
Ink Sketch effect
  about 72
  Coloring adjustment 73
  Ink Outline adjustment 73
Invert Colors feature 63, 64

J

Joint Photographic Experts Group. *See* JPEG
JPEG 18
Julia Fractal 93

L

Lasso Select tool (shortcut key S)
  about 22
  used, for area selecting 52, 53
Layer Properties dialog 103
layers
  adding 100-103
  adjusting 107, 108

  merging 104-106
  moving 109
  working 99
Layers window 16, 100
Levels feature
  about 65
  components 65
  using 66
Line/Curve (shortcut key O) 35

M

MadJik' all plugins 114
Magic Wand tool (shortcut key S)
  about 25
  Flood Mode 26
  used, for area selecting 51, 52
Mandelbrot Fractal 94
menu bar 13
More button 37
Motion Blur effect 77
Move Selected Pixels
    (shortcut key M) 16, 27, 28
Move Selection (shortcut key M) 28, 52
Move tools
  Move Selected Pixels tool 27, 28
  Move Selection tool 28

N

Native Paint.NET. *See* PDN
Noise effects 87

O

Oil Painting effect
  about 73
  Brush Size control 74
  Coarseness control 74
Outline effect
  about 96
  Intensity control 96
  Thickness control 96

P

Paintbrush tool(shortcut key B) 32
Paint Bucket (shortcut key F) 29
  Antialiasing 30
  Blending 30
  Fill setting 30
Paint.NET
  about 5
  Adjustments feature 56
  downloading 6, 7
  improving 115
  installing 6, 7
  photo retouching 38, 39
  plugins 111
  system requirements 5
  tools 21
  URL 6
Paint.NET effects
  artistic 72-74
  blur 74-80
  distort 81-88
  photo 89-91
  Render 91-95
  Stylize 95- 97
Paint.NET file formats
  about 18
  BMP 18
  GIF 18
  JPEG 18
  PDN 19
  PNG 18
  TGA 19
  TIFF 18
Paint.NET help
  Forum 113
  Help Topics (F1) 113
  Tutorials 113
Paint.NET plugins
  BoltBait's plugin pack 114
  dpy's Pack 114
  MadJik' all plugins 114
  obtaining 112, 113
  Photoshop PSD file plugin 114
  Pyrochild plugins 114

Paint.NET plugin types
  Effects 111
  File types 111
Paint.NET tools
  Clone Stamp tool 39-41
  Colors window 37, 38
  Drawing tools 32
  Fill tools 29-31
  Move tools 27, 28
  Photo tools 32-34
  selection tools 22-26
  Shape tools 35, 36
  Text tool 34
  View tools 29
Paint.NET work area
  identifying 12-17
Paint.NET work area windows
  Colors window 15
  History window 17
  image canvas 15
  image list 17
  Layers window 16
  menu bar 13
  status bar 16
  title bar 13
  toolbar 14
Pan tool (shortcut key H) 29
PDN 19
Pencil Sketch effect
  about 74
  Pencil tip size control 74
  Range control 74
Pencil tool(shortcut key P) 32
photo effects
  about 89
  Glow 89
  Red Eye Removal 90
  Sharpen 90
  Soften Portrait 91
Photoshop PSD file plugin 114
Photo tools
  Clone Stamp tool 33
  Color Picker tool 33
  Recolor tool 33
Pixelate effect 83, 84

U

Unfocus effect 79

V

View tools
  Pan tool 29
  Zoom tool 28

W

Windows bitmap. *See* **BMP**

Z

Zoom Blur effect
  about 80
  Center control 80
  Zoom Amount control 80
Zoom tool (shortcut key Z) 28, 52

[PACKT] Thank you for buying
PUBLISHING
Getting Started with Paint.NET

About Packt Publishing

Packt, pronounced 'packed', published its first book *"Mastering phpMyAdmin for Effective MySQL Management"* in April 2004 and subsequently continued to specialize in publishing highly focused books on specific technologies and solutions.

Our books and publications share the experiences of your fellow IT professionals in adapting and customizing today's systems, applications, and frameworks. Our solution based books give you the knowledge and power to customize the software and technologies you're using to get the job done. Packt books are more specific and less general than the IT books you have seen in the past. Our unique business model allows us to bring you more focused information, giving you more of what you need to know, and less of what you don't.

Packt is a modern, yet unique publishing company, which focuses on producing quality, cutting-edge books for communities of developers, administrators, and newbies alike. For more information, please visit our website: www.packtpub.com.

Writing for Packt

We welcome all inquiries from people who are interested in authoring. Book proposals should be sent to author@packtpub.com. If your book idea is still at an early stage and you would like to discuss it first before writing a formal book proposal, contact us; one of our commissioning editors will get in touch with you.

We're not just looking for published authors; if you have strong technical skills but no writing experience, our experienced editors can help you develop a writing career, or simply get some additional reward for your expertise.

Image Processing with ImageJ

ISBN: 978-1-78328-395-8   Paperback: 140 pages

Discover the incredible possibilities of ImageJ, from basic image processing to macro and plugin development

1. Learn how to process digital images using ImageJ and deal with a variety of formats and dimensions, including 4D images.

2. Understand what histograms, region of interest, or filtering means and how to analyze images easily with these tools.

3. Packed with practical examples and real images, with step-by-step instructions and sample code.

Papervision3D Essentials

ISBN: 978-1-84719-572-2   Paperback: 428 pages

Create interactive Papervision3D applications with stunning effects and powerful animations

1. Build stunning, interactive Papervision3D applications from scratch.

2. Export and import 3D models from Autodesk 3ds Max, SketchUp, and Blender to Papervision3D.

3. In-depth coverage of important 3D concepts with demo applications, screenshots, and example code.

Please check **www.PacktPub.com** for information on our titles

Learning Pixelmator

ISBN: 978-1-84969-468-1   Paperback: 118 pages

Enhance your photos effectively and unleash the artist inside, with Pixelmator

1. Learn how to use Pixelmator and its primary tools.

2. Discover how to edit your photos using real-world examples.

3. Use the Effect tools and artistically enhance your images.

SketchBook Pro Digital Painting Essentials

ISBN: 978-1-84969-820-7   Paperback: 112 pages

Create stunning professional grade artwork using Sketchbook Pro

1. Discover tricks and techniques that will help you make the most out of Sketchbook Pro.

2. Packed with practical examples that help you create expressive sketches ranging from cartoons to portraits.

3. A step-by-step guide packed with supporting imagery.

Please check **www.PacktPub.com** for information on our titles